The Phonological Awareness Handbook for Kindergarten and Primary Teachers

Lita Ericson
Mill Woods Public Health Centre
Edmonton, Alberta, Canada

Moira Fraser Juliebö
University of Alberta
Edmonton, Alberta, Canada

International Reading Association
800 Barksdale Road, PO Box 8139
Newark, Delaware 19714-8139, USA
www.reading.org

Director of Publications Joan M. Irwin
Assistant Director of Publications Wendy Lapham Russ
Managing Editor, Books and Electronic Publications Christian A. Kempers
Associate Editor Matthew W. Baker
Assistant Editor Janet S. Parrack
Assistant Editor Mara P. Gorman
Publications Coordinator Beth Doughty
Association Editor David K. Roberts
Production Department Manager Iona Sauscermen
Graphic Design Coordinator Boni Nash
Electronic Publishing Supervisor Wendy A. Mazur
Electronic Publishing Specialist Anette Schütz-Ruff
Electronic Publishing Specialist Cheryl J. Strum
Electronic Publishing Assistant Peggy Mason

Photo Credits Photos by Moira Juliebö. Used with permission. Cover artwork by Dana Whitfield, a student in 1996 at Riverdale Elementary School, Edmonton, Alberta, Canada.

Library of Congress Cataloging in Publication Data
Ericson, Lita.
   The phonological awareness handbook for kindergarten and primary teachers/Lita Ericson, Moira Juliebö.
      p.   cm.
   Includes bibliographical references and index.
   ISBN 0-87207-180-4 (paper:alk. paper)
      1. Phonetics—Study and teaching (Primary)—Handbooks, manuals, etc.
2. Language awareness in children—Handbooks, manuals, etc.
I. Juliebö, Moira.   II. Title.
LB1528.E67   1998   97-51292
372.61—dc21

Fourth Printing, February 2000

This book is dedicated to Ruth, Darryl,
Martin, Austin, and Emily.

Introduction

Language learning is the basis of all communication and the primary instrument of thought. It is an active process that begins at birth and continues throughout life. In their early years, children develop language informally. Long before they understand explicit language rules and conventions, children reproduce the language they learn, and use language to construct and to convey new meaning in unique ways. (Alberta Education, p. 1)

When children enter school their language development is the responsibility of those who teach them. Written language is a powerful means of communication that enables students to access knowledge of the world around them, construct their own knowledge, and share their ideas with others. Research has shown that children who do not succeed in learning to read by Grade 2 have little chance of later success in school (Juel, 1988).

Phonological awareness, awareness of the constituent sounds of words, is a reliable predictor of reading success (Adams, 1990; Blachman, 1989, 1991; Griffith & Olson, 1992; Stanovich, 1986; Yopp, 1995a). Children who have developed the understanding that words can be segmented into sounds tend to be better readers than those with poor phonological awareness ability (Bradley & Bryant, 1983, 1985; Lundberg, Olofsson, & Wall, 1980). Studies also have shown clearly that phonological awareness activities combined with instruction in sound-symbol relations have a significant positive effect on reading and writing ability (Blachman, 1989; Bradley & Bryant,

1983; Hohn & Ehri, 1983). Researchers have demonstrated that activities to enhance phonological awareness can be routinely integrated into daily classroom curriculum (Blachman, 1991). However, at present it is not entirely clear as to what elements of phonological intervention further reading development most effectively. Teachers are struggling with such issues and have the enormous task of selecting activities from current literature. This handbook attempts to aid teachers with this task.

The Phonological Awareness Handbook for Kindergarten and Primary Teachers was developed to provide a practical and comprehensive means of teaching and monitoring children's development of phonological awareness in the classroom. Chapter 1 is a review of pertinent literature to support teaching phonological awareness. Chapter 2 describes lesson plans for a 10-month developmentally appropriate teaching sequence. Chapter 3 presents a teaching program that evaluates students' development of phonological awareness. Chapters 4 through 7 provide a teaching program that includes practice with phonological awareness tasks at levels of increasing difficulty. Chapter 4 is designed to heighten children's appreciation of the sounds in spoken language. The ideas in this chapter are intended to help children enjoy playing with sounds and to build a stronger foundation in sound play and knowledge of rhymes in preparation for higher-level tasks. Chapter 5, extends children's word-play experience and helps them discover sound similarities in spoken language and analyze the component sounds in words. Chapter 6, which presents activities for isolating and categorizing sounds, prepares children for the challenge presented in Chapter 7 on blending and segmenting syllables and sounds. Numerous studies have shown that phonological awareness training programs that include letter-name and letter-sound correspondence instruction have a greater impact on children's reading development than interventions involving phonological awareness or sound-letter instruction alone (Blachman, 1991; Bradley & Bryant, 1983; Hohn & Ehri, 1983). Chapter 8 complements Chapters 3 through 6.

Nicholson (1997) stresses that rich book experiences "at home are not a guarantee of reading and spelling success" (p. 15). Rather, he emphasizes the importance of phonological awareness and letter-sound knowledge. Nicholson recommends that we "introduce phonemic awareness and letter-sound training in kindergarten, so that children from less-privileged backgrounds can start school with competence in these skills" (p. 15).

In order to be effective in promoting reading independence, teachers must incorporate instruction in phonological awareness into meaningful classroom experiences. By embedding entertaining ways to practice sound and word play in a language arts program, teachers can facilitate the growth of readers and writers.

Chapter 1

Frequently Asked Questions About Phonological Awareness

What Is Phonological Awareness?

Phonological awareness refers to the metalinguistic ability that allows children to reflect on features of spoken language (Griffith, Klesius, & Kromrey, 1992). Children who have developed phonological awareness recognize that words can rhyme, can begin or end with the same sound, and are composed of phonemes (sounds) that can be manipulated to create new words. The term phonological awareness encompasses the later developing skill referred to as phonemic awareness, which enables one to consciously reflect on and manipulate sounds to create new words. For example, the letters in *pan* can be rearranged to form the new word *nap* (Hodson, 1994; Stahl, 1992).

When Do Children Develop Phonological Awareness?

Researchers have found data to support that children begin to demonstrate phonological awareness at different ages, and the level of this awareness varies among children (Bradley & Bryant, 1985; Maclean, Bryant, & Bradley, 1987). Children initially acquire a rudimentary understanding that words are independent from meaning and that words are composed of individual sounds. Some children start to make comments on words; for example, "that's a long word"; "those words start the same"; or "those words sound funny" (Schuele & van Kleeck, 1987). By age 3 many children have knowledge of nursery rhymes (Maclean et al., 1987), and other forms of sound play emerge such as alliteration (a pretty pink pig) or nonsense sequences (helicopter–helibopter–helipopter) (van Kleeck & Bryant, 1984). The majority of children, after a year of kindergarten, can generate rhymes, identify syllables, segment words into syllables, and delete the initial syllable of a multisyllabic word (crocodile–croc-odile) (Liberman, Shankweiler, Fischer, & Carter, 1974; Stanovich, Cunningham, & Cramer, 1984; Yopp, 1988). By the end of Grade 1, most children can count and segment or delete phonemes at the beginning of one-, two-, and three-phoneme words in order to generate new words (Pratt & Brady, 1988). However, further research is needed to clearly indicate the developmental acquisition of phonological awareness skills, particularly given the importance of phonological awareness to reading development.

Why Is Phonological Awareness Important to Reading Development?

Phonological awareness is critical to reading development because children who lack phonological awareness are among those most likely to become poor readers (Catts, 1991a; Maclean et al., 1987). Performance on phonological awareness tasks in kindergarten and first grade is related strongly to reading success (Bradley & Bryant, 1983, 1985; Lundberg, Olofsson, & Wall, 1980; Share, Jorm, Maclean, & Matthews, 1984). In fact, phonological awareness is a better predictor of reading achievement than more global measures of general intelligence (IQ tests) or reading readiness (Adams, 1990; Blachman, 1989, 1991; Catts, 1991b; Griffith & Olson, 1992; Stanovich, 1986; Yopp, 1995a).

Phonological awareness affects children's success in reading due to the orthographic nature of the English language, which encodes speech into phonemes (Yopp, 1992). In order to learn to read and spell words, children must understand that spoken words are composed of phonemes that can be manipulated and that these phonemes correspond to letters in written alphabetic script (Ball & Blachman, 1991; Yopp, 1992). Phonological awareness equips children with sufficient understanding of sound structure to capitalize on exposure to print and direct instruction in the relations between letters and sounds (Juel, Griffith, & Gough, 1986).

Why Is Phonological Awareness Difficult for Some Children to Acquire?

As important as phonological awareness is to the process of learning to read, it can be a difficult ability for some children to master (Adams, 1990). Phonological awareness, at its highest level, requires the ability to separate words into independent sounds. But, spectrographic analysis reveals that phonemes in the speech stream are coarticulated with adjacent phonemes and typically are represented in the acoustic signal as syllables (Liberman et al., 1974). Phonemes, then, are abstract and difficult to define in that they are not marked by physical boundaries, and they change as a function of their phonological context. For example, the word *cat* is heard as one acoustic unit rather than as three separate sounds. Given the relative difficulty of phonological awareness tasks that require manipulation of independent sounds, it is important to determine if children have acquired a sufficient understanding of the sound structure of language that they can progress through formal reading instruction.

How Do You Determine Children's Level of Phonological Awareness?

Teachers can use several assessment activities to determine a student's level of phonological awareness. Yopp (1988) cited 10 measures commonly used to assess phonological awareness and compared the reliability, validity, and difficulty of each task. The following tasks were evaluated: sound-to-word matching (Is there a /g/ in *dog*?), word-to-word matching (Do *bat* and *ball* begin the same?), recognition or production of rhyme, isolation of a sound, phoneme segmentation, phoneme counting, phoneme blending, phoneme deletion, specifying deleted phoneme, and phoneme reversal.

Yopp (1988) found evidence that a hierarchical degree of difficulty exists for phonological awareness tasks. Rhyming tasks were the easiest tasks for kindergarten children to perform followed by blending and segmenting; whereas, the most difficult were phoneme deletion tasks. Ball (1993) advocates using tasks in teaching and assessing that are "prerequisite to reading or that contribute to a reciprocal causal relationship to reading" (p. 132). Lewkowicz (1980) stated that the two phonological awareness skills necessary for children to benefit from reading instruction are the abilities to segment and to blend sounds. Furthermore, she argues that tasks requiring manipulation of phonemes appear to be inappropriate for the early stages of phonological awareness training. Griffith and Olson (1992) describe ways to adapt some of the key assessment measures reviewed in Yopp (1988) for classroom use. Practical means and normative guidelines for assessing rhyming ability and blending, isolating, and segmenting phonemes are provided by Griffith and Olson (1992).

Assessing phonological awareness in the classroom can help identify students at risk for reading and spelling difficulty. Once they are identified, a critical question arises: Can phonological awareness be taught to these students?

Can Phonological Awareness Be Taught?

Studies have demonstrated that proper instruction can enhance the development of phonological awareness (Bradley & Bryant, 1983; Gillam & van Kleeck, 1996; Lundberg, Frost, & Petersen, 1988). The impact of this teaching on reading and spelling, however, depends to some extent on the specific components of the phonological awareness instruction.

In an early study, Rosner (1971) found that teaching 4- and 5-year-old children phoneme deletion (for example, say *sun*; now say it again without the *s*) resulted in better word recognition than using traditional classroom reading programs alone. Fox and Routh (1984) reported that kindergartners instructed in both segmenting and blending skills performed significantly better on all tests of sound association and word recognition than children taught in phoneme analysis (segmenting) alone.

Lundberg et al.'s (1988) research involved 235 kindergarten children from 12 classrooms who had not received any previous teaching in letter-sound correspondences. The teaching involved the entire classrooms for 15 to 20 minutes daily in informal exercises and games designed to increase the children's ability to attend to the phonological structure of language. In addition, 155 children from similar classrooms served as a control group and did not receive phonological instruction. The study showed that the children who had received the phonological awareness instruction performed significantly better on measures of spelling ability in Grade 1 and word recognition and spelling ability in Grade 2. Hohn and Ehri (1983) demonstrated that using manipulatives, such as tokens, resulted in improved segmenting skills. Furthermore, they showed that for kindergarten children, those who learned to segment using tokens (see figure) with letters on them performed better on segmenting than the group with unmarked tokens.

Other studies have found that the value of phonological awareness instruction is enhanced when explicit connections are made during training between the printed alphabet symbols and the sound segments in words. In one study, Bradley and Bryant (1983) found important evidence of a causal link between phonological awareness and reading and spelling. They combined rhyme, alliteration, and categorization tasks (oddity tasks in which children had to identify the odd word; for example, bat, cat, sat, ball) to improve the phonological awareness of kindergarten-age children who were nonreaders. The researchers found that reading and spelling skills improved as a result of phonological teaching particularly when explicit instruction in the alphabetic principle was included.

Ball and Blachman's (1991) investigation concluded that kindergarten children can be taught to segment words into their component sounds and that the most successful phonological awareness teaching programs include letter-name and letter-sound instruction that make explicit connections between sound segments and letters. Gillam and van Kleeck's (1996) study involved 16 speech- and language-delayed preschoolers over a 9-month period. Their training focused initially on rhyming tasks and then moved to activities that enhanced awareness of specific phonemes. This research advocates that phonological teaching be included not only for language-impaired children but for those who do not "spontaneously acquire phonological awareness skills during the preschool years" (p. 80). Gillam and van Kleeck's results also suggest that such teaching affects working memory. Furthermore, their research found that rhyming training was effective for their younger subjects (ages 4 to 5 years) and that practice focusing on specific phonemes had direct educational implications for early literacy development.

How Can Phonological Awareness Be Taught in a Classroom Setting?

Although the explicit awareness of the sound structure of language is crucial to the development of reading, activities to facilitate phonological awareness "have not been routinely incorporated into classrooms where beginning reading instruction takes place" (Blachman, 1989, p. 145). Research has shown that phonological awareness activities can be less formal and still result in positive gains in reading and spelling achievement in classroom settings (Lundberg et al., 1988). Phonological awareness can be enhanced through natural and spontaneous ways through the inclusion of word play in stories, songs, and games

(Adams, 1990; Griffith & Olson, 1992), and many phonological awareness skills can be practiced incidentally during routine classroom exercises such as attendance and show and share time. The chapters that follow in this book give many examples of classroom activities that enhance phonological awareness.

Catts (1995) presented seven key factors to consider when teaching phonological awareness:

(1) The level of cognitive-linguistic complexity of phonological awareness varies across activities (recognizing rhymes is easier than generating them);

(2) tasks requiring awareness at the syllable level typically are easier than those requiring awareness at the phoneme level;

(3) phoneme isolation tasks generally are easier than phoneme segmentation tasks;

(4) segmentation or blending tasks are easier with continuant phonemes (e.g., *s*, *sh*, *l*) than with noncontinuant-stop phonemes (e.g., *p*, *b*, *t*) and

(5) segmentation or blending tasks are easier with initial consonants than with final consonants;

(6) manipulatives like disks, tokens, counters, and chips can assist in phoneme segmentation and manipulation tasks; and

(7) phonological awareness activities have a greater impact on reading success when combined with instruction in letter-sound correspondence.

Incorporating strategies to enhance phonological awareness in the classroom is critical to reading success. Griffith, Klesius, and Kromrey (1992) found that the level of phonological awareness that a child possessed upon entering Grade 1 was more important in predicting reading success than the type of instruction (traditional basal or whole language) that they received.

What Are the Implications of These Key Teaching Studies?

Several conclusions can be drawn from the research reviewed in this chapter. First, studies have consistently linked phonological awareness with success in reading and writing

(Bradley & Bryant, 1983, 1985; Gillam & van Kleeck, 1996; Lundberg et al., 1980; Share et al., 1984).

A second conclusion is that kindergarten and first-grade children can benefit from being taught phonological awareness. That is, children who have received this instruction demonstrate a greater awareness of the phonemic segments in words than children who have not received this teaching.

Third, the impact of teaching phonological awareness on reading and spelling is dependent, at least in part, on the specific components of the instruction. Teaching has been more effective when both phoneme analysis and blending are included. Children also are more successful on tasks when manipulatives are used, particularly disks with letters on them.

Finally, studies show that phonological awareness teaching is particularly effective when instruction focuses attention on the relationship between sounds and letters (Cunningham & Cunningham, 1992; Gillam & van Kleeck, 1996).

Summary

The explicit awareness of the sound structure of language is the most accurate predictor of reading achievement cited in the research literature. Many children have difficulty understanding that in the English orthographic system words are composed of individual phonemes and that these phonemes correspond to letters in written alphabetic script. Early identification of children with weak phonological awareness skills may help prevent some reading disabilities. However, all students can benefit from the inclusion of phonological activities in instructional planning. By incorporating activities to facilitate phonological awareness into a meaningful language arts program, teachers can help children to develop as successful readers and writers.

Chapter 2

A Teaching Sequence: Diagnostic Measures and Teaching Activities

The remainder of this handbook provides a sequence for phonological awareness development. How these activities are implemented, of course, depends on the learning and developmental levels of individual children. Some tasks can be performed in small- and large-group settings. If the tasks are presented at an appropriate level of difficulty, they are more likely to be enjoyed. Students should be limited to oral activities until they know the alphabet letters (Hohn & Ehri, 1983; Yopp, 1992). In some instances, children will require one-to-one individual instruction, whereas at other times they may be grouped for appropriate instruction, but most of the activities in this book are intended to enrich the language development of all children in the class.

It is recommended, that when needed, teachers spend some daily instructional time teaching phonological awareness. However, many of the activities provided may already be part of regular Kindergarten and Grade 1 classroom curriculum.

Students who have poorly developed phonological awareness will require consistent and intentional incorporation of these activities into everyday classroom language exercises. These activities will facilitate the reading and spelling ability of all children. For some children these phonological awareness activities will enhance the natural rapid progress of literacy development, for others they may help prevent reading and spelling difficulties, and for others the activities may help reduce the degree of impairment of a reading disability.

Phonological Awareness Activities

The following list provides an example of how phonological awareness activities can be incorporated into daily classroom activities.

1. Decide which phonological awareness skills to measure such as rhyming, blending, segmenting, and orthographic knowledge.

2. Administer some or all of the diagnostic activities found in the Appendixes. (Directions for administering the four pre- and postteaching measures can be found in Chapter 3. Forms to record and score responses are provided in Appendixes 2–9).

3. Introduce a nursery rhyme, poem, song, finger play, or story with alliteration or rhyme at the beginning of each week. (For examples of suitable selections, see Chapters 4, 7, and Appendix 1.)

4. Write the selection in a Big Book.

5. Send home a copy of the selection at the beginning of the week.

6. Read daily the selection of the week with the class.

7. Choose daily an activity from the chapter that you are working on currently.

8. Ensure that daily activities incorporate letter-sound teaching (see Chapter 8 for further activities for letters and sounds).

9. Evaluate growth at the end of the 8-month teaching program by administering the applicable postteaching tests. (Appendixes 6–9 provide response score sheets for measuring growth.)

Teaching Time Lines: A 10-Month Calendar

The phonological awareness activities in this handbook are designed to be embedded in every day classroom routines. However, some activities are more difficult and are mastered by some children at later developmental stages. The teaching time line presented here provides an example of how to measure and teach the phonological awareness activities in a developmentally appropriate sequence recognizing that some months are more consistent in routine than others.

September

1. Decide which phonological awareness skills to measure (rhyming, blending, segmenting, or orthographic knowledge).

2. Administer some or all of the diagnostic measures. (Directions for administering the four diagnostic measures can be found in Chapter 3. Forms to record and score responses are provided in the Appendixes.)

3. Send parents the letter found in Chapter 4 when you begin the chapter.

4. Select one rhyme, poem, finger play, or story at the beginning of the each week. (For examples, see Chapter 4 or Appendix 1.) Record this selection in a Big Book. (If it is a story, you may want to record only part of it: the book title, author, and one example of rhyming or alliteration.) By the end of this 8-month teaching program, you should have about 30 selections recorded. Send a copy of the rhyme or a brief description of the selection to the parents.

5. Sing the "Alphabet Song" frequently (see Chapter 8).

6. Choose one activity daily from Chapter 4.

7. Encourage children to recite or share their favorite rhyme, poem, or story at the end of the month.

October and November

1. Send parents a copy of the letter found in Chapter 5 when you begin that chapter.

2. Select one rhyme, poem, finger play, or story at the beginning of each week. (For examples, see Chapter 4 or Appendix 1.) Record this selection in a Big Book. (If it is a story, you may want to record the book title, author, and one example of rhyming or alliteration.) Also send a copy of the rhyme or a brief description of the selection to the parents.

3. Choose one activity daily from Chapter 5.

4. Ensure that activities to enhance letter-sound association are included in Rhyme Time planning (see Chapter 8).

5. Have all children recite or share their favorite rhyme, poem, or story throughout these months.

December, January, and February

1. Send parents a copy of the letter found in Chapter 6 when you begin activities in that chapter.

2. Select one rhyme, poem, finger play, or story at the beginning of each week. (For examples, see Chapter 6 or Appendix 1.) Record this selection in a Big Book. (If it is a story, you may want to record the book title, author, and one example of rhyming or alliteration.) Send a copy of the rhyme or a brief description of the selection to the parents.

3. Choose one activity daily from Chapter 6.

4. Ensure that activities to enhance letter-sound associations are included in teaching activities (see Chapter 8.)

5. Have children recite or share their favorite rhyme, poem, or story throughout these months.

March, April, May, and June

1. Send parents a copy of the letter found in Chapter 7 when you begin the activities in that chapter.

2. Select one rhyme, poem, finger play, or story at the beginning of each week. (See Chapter 7 and Appendix 1.)

3. Record this selection in a Big Book. (If it is a story, you may want to record the book title, author, and one example of rhyming or alliteration.)

4. Send parents a copy of the rhyme or a brief description of the selection.

5. Choose one activity daily from Chapter 7.

6. Ensure that programming includes letter-sound association training (see Chapter 8).

7. Have children recite or share their favorite rhyme, poem, or story throughout each month.

8. Readminister the diagnostic measures that were given preteaching at the end of the 8-month teaching program. (Appendixes 6–9 provide response score sheets for postteaching testing.)

Preparing Lessons in Phonological Awareness

Teachers are in an ideal position to develop and reinforce phonological awareness skills in ways that are functional and fun and that make sense within the context of classroom themes and focus of instruction. Teachers can ensure that the students are successful by making the tasks consistent with the students' cognitive and linguistic abilities and responding enthusiastically to students' attempts to manipulate language. With help, children can achieve learning that they could not manage on their own (see Vygotsky, 1962). By having new learnings mediated, the child is able to obtain maximum benefit from direct interactions with the environment. The mediator communicates with the child, is aware of the child's response, and through these interactions, the child learns meaningful thinking strategies that may be applied in future situations. When children are consistently praised for their success, they develop feelings of competence as learners (Feuerstein & Mentzkar, 1993). In addition, the teacher can create phonological awareness activities and letter-sound exercises, which parents can use to reinforce phonological awareness activities at home.

Ultimately, the goal of teaching phonological awareness is to enable students to understand that words can be separated into component sounds (Yopp, 1992). Teaching, however, can be successful only if tasks are presented at an appropriate level of difficulty. Consideration of the following key questions can assist teachers in planning lessons to ensure students' success.

1. Can the task be performed successfully at the receptive level? For example, is the student able to pick an object that starts with /t/? If so, have the student work at the expres-

sive level. For example, the student can name two words that start with the same sound.

2. Is the nature of the phonological awareness task too difficult for the students? That is, do they have knowledge of rhymes? If so, can they generate rhymes? At a more difficult level, can they isolate sounds? Can they group words based on similarities among sounds at the beginning, middle, and end of words? Can they blend together sounds to make words or break apart words to make sounds? And, at the highest level of difficulty, can the students manipulate the sounds to make new words? How can the task be scaffolded if the child has difficulties?

3. Is this level of phonological awareness too easy for the students? Can they already segment sentences? If so, use words. If they can segment words, then use syllables. If they can segment syllables, then work at the most difficult level of phonemes.

4. Can the students perform these tasks with initial consonants? If so, try final consonants. If tasks can be performed with final consonants, try working with sounds in the middle of words.

5. Can the students segment and blend continuants (*f*, *v*, *sh*, *s*, *z*, *th*) and vowels? If so, try stop consonants (*p*, *b*, *t*, *d*, *k*, *g*).

6. Do the students have some knowledge of letter-sound correspondences? If so, introduce some plastic or foam letters.

7. Can the students perform tasks with simple consonant-vowel (CV) or vowel-consonant (VC) sequences? If so, progress to consonant-vowel-consonant (CVC) combinations (*cat*) and eventually work with more complex consonant and vowel combinations (CCVC) (*star*).

Phonological awareness activities should not be taught in isolation, but rather should be an integral part of the reading and writing process. Children need to be exposed to and interact with a collection of literacy materials that is rich and varied. It is essential that they develop a positive attitude toward literacy events and a strong motivation to read and write. Furthermore, children need to observe and participate with skilled readers and writers, practice strategies with support, and read independently.

Chapter 3

Monitoring Progress

As mentioned in previous chapters, the early identification of students with poor phonological awareness may help prevent reading problems in some children. This chapter provides information for identifying such children. This can include warning signs from their past and present behaviors. This chapter also presents several tools that can serve both for identification and monitoring purposes.

There are three main factors that may place a student at higher risk for phonological awareness deficiency (Catts, 1995): (1) family history of reading disabilities, (2) phonological deficits, and (3) language problems that persist past age 5. In addition, students who may be at risk for phonological awareness deficits normally show one or more of the following warning signs. The child

- does not comprehend or enjoy rhymes or books;
- has trouble detecting or producing rhyming words or patterns of alliteration (recognizing that words may begin with the same sound);
- has problems breaking words into syllables or sounds (cannot tap out the number of syllables in a word);
- has trouble identifying where a sound is positioned in a word (beginning, middle, or end);
- cannot blend sounds to make a word;
- has difficulty clapping hands or tapping feet in rhythm with songs and rhymes;

- has difficulty in learning sound-letter correspondences; and

- lacks an awareness of speech sounds.

Pre- and postteaching tests have been designed to measure four main skills: rhyme detection, blending, segmenting, and orthographic knowledge. These diagnostic tests should be administered prior to teaching the activities in Chapters 4–8. The postteaching tests can be administered after completing the phonological teaching program.

Rhyme detection is a rudimentary phonological awareness skill that children typically can perform at age 3 or 4 (Maclean et al., 1987). Blending was chosen because it is a relatively easy task focusing on a higher level of phonological awareness. Although the third measure, segmentation, is a very difficult task, it was chosen because it is a good predictor of decoding readiness. The fourth task, an invented spelling measure, was chosen because it is used frequently to measure written orthographic knowledge (Robertson & Salter, 1995; Swank & Catts, 1994).

Teachers can decide which measures to administer before and after teaching. These four skills can each be tested independently or together with a total administration time of about 25 minutes. Test administration can be performed by a teacher, trained assistant, or parent volunteer.

Step 1: Directions Preteaching Test: Rhyme Detection

1. Administer this phonological awareness test prior to beginning activities in Chapter 4. This test should be administered to each student individually by a teacher, assistant, or parent volunteer in a relatively quiet setting with minimal distractions (see Appendixes 2 and 6).

2. Explain that rhymes are words that have endings that sound the same.

3. Demonstrate examples of words that rhyme and words that do not rhyme.

4. Make a list consisting of 20 pairs of common words. Select rhyming pairs (such as *bat–cat*) for a least 50 percent of the pairs. Try to choose words with which children in your classroom are familiar.

Teacher: Rhymes are words that sound the same at the end. *Bat* rhymes with *cat; man* rhymes with *can.* Does *ball* rhyme with *tall?* Yes, *ball* rhymes with *tall.* Not all words rhyme. Does *book* rhyme with *cup.* No, *book* and *cup* do not rhyme because *book* ends with *ook* and *cup* ends with *up.* Does *all* rhyme with *tall?* Yes. Now I am going to say some words, and I want you to tell me if they rhyme.

1. dad–sad	11. me–see
2. set–get	12. game–can
3. head–bed	13. want–went
4. cook–bee	14. joy–boy
5. eat–seat	15. moon–soon
6. farm–car	16. say–may
7. been–seen	17. snow–cold
8. come–mom	18. cake–make
9. cow–bird	19. store–more
10. flower–power	20. light–night

Score:_____/20

This task was an adaptation of a test described in Yopp (1988), which was originally designed by Calfee, Chapman, and Venezky (1972). Yopp reported that kindergarten children scored a mean of 14 out of 20 on this task and that it took approximately 1 to 2 minutes to administer. The Yopp rhyme test had a reliability of .78.

Step 2: Directions for Preteaching Test: Blending

1. Administer this phonological awareness test at the beginning and at the end of the 8-month teaching period. This test

should be administered to each student individually by a teacher, assistant, or parent volunteer (see Appendixes 3 and 7).

2. Create a list of 30 short words. The first 10 words should have two phonemes that are segmented into two parts (such as a-t); the second 10 words should each have three or four phonemes that are segmented into two parts (such as b-ag, st-op); and the third set of 10 words should consist of words that are three to four phonemes in length and can be segmented into three parts (such as b-a-g, st-o-p).

3. Ask the child to guess what word you are saying. (For example, c-ar, What word did I say?)

1.	i–s	16.	c–at
2.	d–o	17.	s–eat
3.	b–e	18.	st–ep
4.	i–t	19.	m–ine
5.	m–y	20.	s–it
6.	t–o	21.	d–o–g
7.	o–n	22.	b–a–g
8.	s–ee	23.	c–u–p
9.	u–p	24.	s–i–ck
10.	i–n	25.	b–oo–k
11.	m–om	26.	c–oa–t
12.	c–ut	27.	m–a–n
13.	h–ead	28.	f–i–ve
14.	b–all	29.	w–a–sh
15.	l–eg	30.	h–ea–t

Score:____/30

This task was an adaptation of the Roswell-Chall Test of Auditory Blending (1959), as described in Yopp (1988). Yopp reported that kindergarten children scored a mean of 20 out of 30 correct responses on this task and that it took approximately 5 to 10 minutes to administer. This phoneme blending test had a reliability rating of .96 when it was used in Yopp's study.

Blending was reported to be a more difficult task than rhyming but an easier task than segmenting (Blachman,

1991). Kamhi (1992) stated that blending three- and four-phoneme words was an appropriate task for 4-year-olds.

Step 3: Directions for Preteaching Test: Segmenting

1. Administer this test at the beginning and at the end of the 8-month teaching period. This test should be administered to each student individually by a teacher, assistant, or parent volunteer (see Appendixes 4 and 8).

2. Select 22 common words (two to three sounds in length).

3. Choose words made up of a variety of consonant sounds and vowels. Try to pick words that the child has in his or her vocabulary (familiar words based on background experiences).

4. Demonstrate how words can be segmented into sounds. Say "I have a special language that I want to teach you. In this language, words are said in a special way. Words are broken apart and each sound is said separately. For example, the word *up* is said /u//p/. The word *dog* is said like /d//o//g/. The word *duck* is said like /d//u//k/. Now it is your turn to try. Say *seat*. Right /s//ea//t/. After giving this explanation, try the following test.

1.	is	12.	no
2.	cat	13.	boy
3.	men	14.	sit
4.	to	15.	in
5.	car	16.	do
6.	bee	17.	leg
7.	sun	18.	on
8.	if	19.	cup
9.	ball	20.	yes
10.	so	21.	me
11.	pen	22.	won

Score:____/22

Yopp (1988) found that children in April and May of the kindergarten year achieved a mean score of 12 out of 22. Although mean scores were low, this segmentation task was found to be reliable and a good predictor of readiness for explicit instruction in decoding (Griffith et al., 1992; Yopp, 1988).

Step 4: Directions for Preteaching Test: Invented Spelling

Note that this test is a preview or review and is to be used qualitatively to show a child's growth over a school year. For grade scores use a standardized spelling test.

1. Administer this test at the beginning and at the end of the 8-month teaching period. This test should be administered to each student individually by a teacher, assistant, or parent volunteer (see Appendixes 5 and 9).

2. Select 20 words from a list of words suitable for Kindergarten or Grade 1 children. For example, see Larsen and Hammill's (1994) *Test of Written Spelling*; Tarasoff's (1990) *Spelling Strategies You Can Teach*; Fry, Fountoukidis, and Polk's (1985) *The New Reading Teacher's Book of Lists*; or Sitton's (1996) *Spelling Sourcebook 1*.

3. Say the word. Say it in a sentence. Repeat the word. Encourage approximations: "Try to write as much of the word as you can. Some words are hard. I will say the words slowly. What can you hear?" Rate the child's spelling according to one of the four stages in Robertson and Salter (1995). For example: "way spelt wos" is at stage 3.

Stage 1
Prerepresentational: No logical representation of sounds (house = ip).
Stage 2
Developmental: Logical representation of some sounds (house = how).
Stage 3
Representational: Logical representation of most sounds (house = hows).

Stage 4
Conventional: Logical representation of essentially
                       all sounds (house = house).

Count how many words fit each stage and enter the numbers in the boxes on the chart, which will show the stage that most characterizes the child's spelling.

Emily: Grade 1.   September

Stage 1	Stage 2	Stage 3	Stage 4
6	12	2	0

Conclusion

By examining phonological awareness abilities using both qualitative (family history) and quantitative measures, students at risk for reading difficulties may be identified and specific programming for phonological awareness can then be implemented.

Chapter 4

Fun With Sounds

This chapter is designed to increase children's appreciation of the sounds in spoken language. Experiences with language and exposure to literacy events in the classroom help to facilitate phonological awareness, but many children need more explicit training (Adams, 1990; Blachman, 1991). Ideas in this chapter contribute to the joy of playing with sounds and build a stronger foundation in sound play and knowledge of rhymes in preparation for higher level phonological awareness tasks. Sound play provides an opportunity to focus on the structure of language without having to attend to its meaning (Yopp, 1995b).

The first part of this chapter, Listening for Sounds, focuses on receptive tasks and presents creative ideas for children to listen to rhymes, poems, finger plays, television jingles, or stories that contain rhyme, alliteration, or nonsense sequences. As their awareness and familiarity with rhyme develops, children can participate in the second part, Playing With Sounds, which focuses on expressive tasks.

Listening for Sounds (Receptive)

The following activities provide practice in listening for environmental sounds and for sound play in language and will help prepare children for the expressive activities.

Listening for Environmental Sounds

1. Sit in a circle with the class with a bag of objects that make noise (for example, a horn or bell). Have a child remove

an object from the bag and demonstrate the sound it makes. The other children who have their eyes closed must guess which object is making the sound.

2. Take children outside and have them listen for different sounds. Later, make a list of the sounds that were heard outside. Students also can take turns describing sounds.

3. Listen to a tape of environmental sounds.

4. Have children move to various drum rhythms.

Listening for Word and Sound Play

1. Have children listen to nursery rhymes, poems, finger plays, television jingles, and songs or stories that contain rhyming (*cat* and *hat*), alliteration (*large lazy lions lounging*), or nonsense sequences (*tri ya yangle*) (van Kleeck & Bryant, 1984). It is important to share the joy of reading selections that have language play as a major component. The enthusiasm that you model is contagious.

2. Recite nursery rhymes and poems aloud repeating the rhymes, which will help children learn sound and word patterns. Nursery rhymes or stories such as *Hop on Pop* (Seuss, 1965) and *There's a Wocket in My Pocket* (Seuss, 1974) are excellent for increasing children's awareness. *When a Bear Bakes a Cake* (Tomkins, 1987) demonstrates rhyming, repetition, and manipulation of phonemes in an entertaining and memorable way.

3. Highlight word play in a selection by drawing attention to the words within phrases and the sounds within words. For example, the teacher might ask, "Did you hear all the words that rhymed?" or "Did you enjoy listening to all the funny words and sounds in this book?"

Playing With Sounds (Expressive)

The following guidelines for encouraging class participation using nursery rhymes, other rhymes, poems, games, songs, and stories with rhymes, alliteration, and nonsense sound sequences were derived from the authors' own experiences and from a review of several training studies (Ball & Blachman, 1991; Bradley et al., 1983, 1985; Hohn & Ehri, 1983; Lundberg et al., 1988) and related articles (Yopp, 1995b).

1. Record the children's examples of rhyming, alliteration, or nonsense sequences in a Big Book. Record the selection of the short rhyme, poem, or song in the Big Book as well. If the selection is too long, record only the title, author, and an example of alliteration or rhyme from the story.

2. Read the selection twice to the children.

3. Highlight word play in the selection. For example, the teacher might ask, "Did you hear all the words that rhymed?" or "Did you enjoy listening to all the funny words and sounds in this book?"

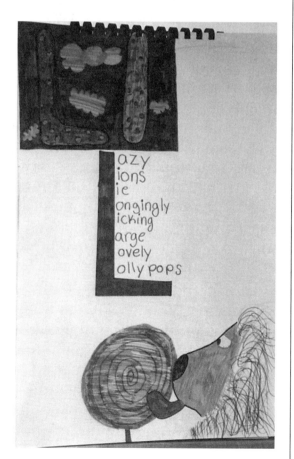

Examples of alliteration recorded in a Big Book.

4. Encourage students to comment on the word play in the selection. For example, the teacher could ask, "What did you like about the book?"

5. Draw attention to the structure of language, like the words within phrases or sentences and the sounds within words. Have the children divide sentences into increasingly smaller parts or play with the order of the words in sentences. Show them that the meaning of the word is separate from its length.

6. Talk about phonemic features. For example, the teacher might make comments like "those words start with the same sound *kuh, k-k-k-cake, k-k-k-car, k-k-k-cat*."

7. Encourage predictions by having students predict sounds, words, or phrases in selections and then have them explain how they formulated their predictions (Yopp, 1992).

8. Create additional verses or have students make up their own version of a selection or story: such as *Humpty Dumpty was very tall, Humpty Dumpty went to the mall.* It is not necessary that children generate responses that rhyme. This exercise will help children realize that the structure of language is manipulable.

In the following sections, specific activities for facilitating awareness of the sound similarities in spoken language through participation in word and sound play are presented. A variety of mediums are discussed, including: games, nursery rhymes, rhymes, and poems; songs and music; drama; art; and stories and writing. Early examples of sound play may include nonsense rhyme and alliteration, adding word endings, spontaneous playing with or practicing the pronunciation of a word, and commenting on or attracting attention to pronunciations. At a higher level of phonological awareness, play also might include segmenting words into individual syllables or sounds (Schuele & van Kleeck, 1987).

Activities Using Games

1. Have children clap the syllables in their name as attendance is taken. The teacher can call out first or last names.

2. Clap out the syllables in the day of the week (*Fri–day*) or in the description of the weather (*sun–ny* or *win–dy*).

3. Have children match words and syllables to physical movements such as clapping, marching, and walking. The rhythmic activities help the children focus on speech segments.

Activities Using Nursery Rhymes, Rhymes, and Poems

1. Encourage recitation or memorization of a poem, rhyme, or riddle. This familiarity gives children the confidence needed to change words and make the rhymes their own. Begin with well-known nursery rhymes. Maclean et al. (1987) found that the five most popular nursery rhymes are "Humpty Dumpty," "Baa-Baa Black Sheep," "Hickory Dickory Dock," "Jack and Jill," and "Twinkle, Twinkle, Little Star."

2. Clap out the words in a nursery rhyme or poem (Geor–gie Por–gie pud–ding and pie…).

3. Draw children's attention to funny phrases or pronunciations of words or sounds ("Peter Piper picked a peck of pickled peppers—That's hard to say").

4. Try word substitution play with familiar rhymes such as "Mary Had a Little Lamb"—Mary had a little house, or Mary had a little cow. The ability to perform word substitution play was documented as early as age 3½ by van Kleeck and Bryant (1984).

Activities Using Songs and Music

1. March to rhymes or other sound play selections. Songs that have only one beat per word like "Baa-Baa Black Sheep" facilitate rhyming ability and word awareness.

2. Set up a music center that focuses on phonological awareness. This center can be used in a variety of ways.

- A tape recorder can be placed at the center with a variety of songs and rhymes recorded. "Mary Had a Little Lamb," "Baa-Baa Black Sheep," "Old McDonald Had a Farm," and "Jack and Jill" or audio books like *Each Peach Pear Plum* (Ahlberg & Ahlberg, 1978) could be played. Children could sit in a circle and clap out the number of syllables in the words in the song or rhyme selection.

- Lead the children in a chant of a favorite nursery rhyme or song. The rhyme selection could be written on a paper flip chart to help cue the children.
- Children could take turns leading the activity.

- Musical instruments could be placed around the circle with a card labeling or depicting the instrument or sound to be used at each spot (for example, a tambourine, a pot with a wooden dowel, two wooden dowels, fingers snapping, bell, drum, hands clapping, xylophone, or feet tapping). Part of a song could be played on the tape recorder. When the tape recorder is stopped, children could rotate places. Also, children could try to finish saying or singing the part of the song that was not played.

3. Have fun adding or deleting words in songs. For instance, have students select the animal to sing about in "Old McDonald Had a Farm"—"And on his farm he had a tyrannosaurus rex."

4. You can make up songs based on familiar rhymes. For instance to the tune of "Here We Go Round the Mulberry Bush":

Jack and Jill go up the hill,
up the hill, up the hill;
Jack and Jill go up the hill
to fetch a pail of water.
Jack falls down and breaks his crown,
breaks his crown, breaks his crown;
Jack falls down and breaks his crown
and Jill comes tumbling after.

5. Adapt lyrics to familiar songs like "Six White Ducks":

Five little fish that I once knew,
fat fish, skinny fish, fair ones too.
But the one little fish
with a fin on his back,
He led the others with his flip, flop, flip,

Flip, flop, flip.
Flip, flop, flip.
He led the others with his flip, flop, flip.

6. Sing songs that already contain rhymes like "Twinkle, Twinkle Little Star."

Activities Using Drama

1. Have children mime their favorite nursery rhyme and have their classmates try to guess the rhyme.

2. Recite a nursery rhyme chorally with the class and have small groups of children take turns miming the rhyme.

3. Assign a small group of children to the characters in a well-known nursery rhyme. Have the rest of the class interview those characters about what happened in the rhyme. For example in "Jack and Jill," ask Why did Jack fall down? Did Jack and Jill go for water everyday?

Reciting and miming a rhyme.

Activities Using Art

1. Have children illustrate their favorite nursery rhyme or nursery rhyme character.

2. Create a bulletin board of characters from nursery rhymes.

3. Let children view a picture of a nursery rhyme and have them guess the rhyme.

4. Have children make puppets to illustrate a nursery rhyme or a book such as *Little Miss Muffet* or *The Paper Bag Princess* (Munsch, 1980).

Activities Using Stories and Writing

1. Clap out the words to a frequently repeated sentence in a fairy tale. For example, from "The Three Bears," "Someone's been eating my porridge" (Sawyer, 1988).

2. Use books with lots of predictability, repetition, alliterative patterns, and rhyme that play with sounds through rhyme and the manipulation of sounds (Griffith et al., 1992; Yopp, 1995b). Books such as *Goodnight Moon* (Brown & Hurd, 1975) and *Chicken Soup With Rice* (Sendak, 1991) serve as excellent resources to focus on rhyme. The play with sounds and sound patterns in stories needs to be explicit, "their structures readily accessible, and their content simple enough that the stories can be extended" (Yopp, 1995b, p. 538). In this article, Yopp provides an excellent annotated bibliography of read-aloud books for developing phonological awareness. Some examples listed in this resource list are as follows:

> Cameron, P. (1961). *"I can't," said the ant*. New York: Coward-McCann.
>
> In this story household items discuss the fall of a teapot from the counter in a kitchen and the means by which to put it back. In a series of brief contributions to the conversation, each item says something that rhymes with its own name. "'Don't break her,' said the shaker," and "'I can't bear it,' said the carrot." (p. 539)
>
> Hague, K. (1984). *Alphabears*. New York: Henry Holt.
>
> In this beautifully illustrated book, 26 teddy bears introduce the alphabet and make use of alliteration: "Teddy bear John loves jam and jelly." (p. 539)

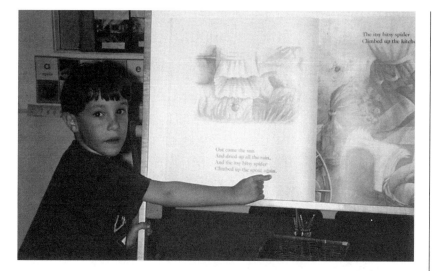

Pointing out the rhyme in *The Itsy Bitsy Spider* (Traponi, 1993). Reprinted with permission of Whispering Coyote Press.

3. Point out rhymes in books such as *Brown Bear, Brown Bear* (Carle, 1992) and *The Itsy Bitsy Spider* (Traponi, 1993). Drawing attention to the rhyme increases the saliency of the rhyme and consequently improves students' ability to notice the rhymes themselves.

Conclusion

By focusing on receptive tasks through listening to rhymes, poems, stories, and environmental sounds, we provide experiences that will help children with expressive tasks.

About the Parent Letter and Lesson Plan

The parent letter is designed to encourage parents to engage in a variety of activities to further their child's reading and writing development.

The sample lesson plan, which illustrates how activities that increase awareness and familiarity with sounds and letters, can be integrated into the daily routines of the classroom.

Parent Letter

Dear Family,

Read aloud as often as possible with your child. Let your child choose the book most of the time. [Share your enthusiasm for books and have fun!]

Talk about the book with your child, pointing out the title and author. Ask questions about the book or story: What do you think is going to happen next? Encourage your child to ask questions and take time to answer these questions.

Sing the "Alphabet Song" ("A, B, C, D....Z, now I know my A, B, C's, next time won't you sing with me"). Point out letters around the house (on cereal boxes, in the telephone book, on television, or in magazines).

Recite familiar rhymes like "Jack and Jill," "Twinkle, Twinkle Little Star," "Mary Had a Little Lamb," "Little Miss Muffet," "Humpty Dumpty," "Baa-Baa Black Sheep," "Old Mother Hubbard," and "Hickory Dickory Dock."

Sample Lesson Plan for September

1. Teacher claps syllables in students' first name as she takes attendance (Rita–2 claps).
2. Sing the "Alphabet Song" (that is, "A, B, C, D,...Z, now I know my A, B, C's, next time won't you sing with me").
3. Introduce the sound /f/. Provide auditory, visual, and kinesthetic feedback on how to produce /f/.
4. Sing the song "Five Little Fish." Draw attention to the rhyming words in the song.

Chapter 5

Rhyme Time

As was discussed in Chapter 4, word play in the form of games, rhymes, poems and riddles, songs, and stories help children to discover sound similarities in spoken language (Liberman et al., 1974). Most children, even those for whom English is a second language, enjoy rhyme with its cadence and rhythmic repetitive phrases. Maclean et al. (1987) found that performance on rhyme and alliteration detection tasks was related to success in beginning reading. Rhyming words are identical except for onset, which is the part of the word that comes before the stressed vowel (Calfee et al., 1972, as cited in Lewkowicz, 1980). Through rhyme and manipulation of phonemes in alliteration and assonance, the same sound occurs in two or more words of text.

In the previous chapter, students were provided with background experience in listening for environmental sounds to build their awareness of word and sound play in spoken language. As children's familiarity with rhymes, alliteration, and nonsense sequences develop, they are able to engage in rhyme, alliteration, and sound judgment tasks, which in turn help them to analyze the component sounds in words (Lundberg et al., 1988; Maclean et al., 1987).

Activities Using Rhyming, Alliteration and Nonsense Sequences, and Sound Judgment

Rhyming

The rhyming tasks have been divided into three levels of complexity (knowledge, discrimination, and production) listed from least difficult (receptive activities) to most difficult (expressive tasks).

Knowledge of rhyme (receptive)

1. Determine if pairs of words rhyme (Do the words *cat* and *bat* rhyme?).

2. Play games like "Red Rover, Red Rover, we call Susan over." Have fun modifying the words to the game; for example, "Dear Clyde, dear Clyde, we call John to our side"; "My dear, my dear, we call Terry over here."

3. Use guessing games as a means for drawing children's attention to rhymes. Teachers can play I Spy rhyme play by using pictures that are full of rhyming pairs (a dog and a frog; a hook and a book) or by using books like *Moose on the Loose* (Ochs, 1991).

Discrimination of rhyme (receptive)

1. Teach children to categorize or group together pictures of real objects on the basis of shared sounds. *Hat* could be grouped with *bat* and *rat*, because they share the same end sounds.

2. Play rhyme oddity games. For example, Which word does not belong: *sat/mat/bat/sun*; *feet/cat/meet*?

3. Play sound matching games. Play rhyming charades and have students act out two words that rhyme; play Go Fish or Memory in small groups with rhyming pairs.

4. Have children choose objects from a bag and indicate whether the objects rhyme or not (*bat, can, fan, frog, pan*). If the activity is played in a large group, several bags of objects can be used. This activity could be modified to emphasize a particular sound: Children could take turns choosing objects and indicating whether they start with the targeted sound.

Production of rhyme (expressive)

1. Play an introduction game, such as *My name is _____ and I like _____.* (My name is Lita and I like pita.)

2. Other games like Simon Says also could be adapted. The task *Simon says say a word that rhymes with ball* could be simplified by providing more cues or information: *Simon says say a word that rhymes with ball; I'll give you a hint, I'm very t____* .

3. Have children make up rhyming words about a particular topic theme. For example, outdoor words—*fun, sun, run; hide, ride, slide.*

4. Have children tell you words that rhyme. *Tell me a word that rhymes with hop.*

5. Play a guessing game. (*This word rhymes with pop and bunny rabbits do this, they ____.*) You could simplify this task by choosing words within a theme such as animals. Catts and Vartiainen (1993) list several similar sentences to generate rhymes. For example, *A fish named Jim, was learning to ____* (p. 43).

6. Have students sit in a circle. The teacher starts this activity by holding a rhyming ball. She says a word (such as *ball*) and then tosses the ball to a student who has to say a word that rhymes (*hall*). Then the student tosses the ball to another student who has to think of another word that rhymes (*all*). Lists of words that are easy to play rhyming games with are found in Appendix 1.

7. Present pictures or objects and have children generate as many words as they can that rhyme with the presented stimuli.

Alliteration and Nonsense Sequences

1. Enjoy sharing other types of nonsense sound play like *David says go, Sarah says ogo, Peter says pogo.* Children enjoy hearing their name in sound play.

2. Play with alliterative sequences—*mama mee mee mow mow moo moo, my dada dee dee dow dow do do.*

3. Determine if pairs are alliterative. Do *dad/door* or *bat/shoe* start with the same sound?

Sound Judgment

1. Expose children to words that are different in length and have them give examples of short and long words.

Clapping out syllables in words.

Objects can be used to help children learn that word length is separate from word meaning. Listen for changes in the length of words as affixes are added or deleted (*run/running, happy/happiness, tie/untie*) (Sawyer, 1988).

2. Have children judge word length (for example, Which sounds longer—*snake/caterpillar, cup/bicycle*?).

3. Have children decide whether pairs contain the same number of syllables (for example, How many claps are there in the words but–ter–fly and el–e–phant?).

Activities Using Nursery Rhymes, Other Rhymes, and Poems

1. Use a selection loaded heavily with pairs of rhyming words and use peelable sticky notes to cover the rhyming pair so the children can guess it. For example, use "Humpty Dumpty":

> Humpty Dumpty sat on a wall
> Humpty Dumpty had a great _____;

All the king's horses and all the king's men
Couldn't put Humpty together _____.

2. Use rhymes that emphasize specific syllables; (for example, *Ee–nie, Mee–nie, Min–nie, Mo*).

3. Ask children if they can recite any nursery rhymes. Then suggest a rhyme and encourage children to suggest the missing rhyming words in the passage; for example, "Do you know 'Jack and Jill'?"

Jack and Jill
went up the _____ .

Use this experience to develop the children's metacognitive awareness of rhyme. Use substitutions like *street* for *hill* to encourage monitoring.

Activities Using Songs and Music

1. Sing songs that contain rhyming, alliteration, or nonsense sequences. For example, children can sing "The Name Game":

Dean Dean bo bean, banana bana bo bean, fee fie fo fean,
Dee–an;
Sara Sara bo bara, banana bana bo bara, fee fie fo fara, Sa–ra.

Some other examples of songs are "This Old Man," "Three Little Monkeys," "I Caught a Fish Alive," "Row, Row, Row Your Boat," "A Hunting We Will Go," "The Wheels On the Bus," "Roll Over," and the following song, "The Ants Go Marching:"

The ants go marching one by one,
Hurrah, hurrah.
The ants go marching one by one,
Hurrah, hurrah.
The ants go marching one by one,
The little one stops to suck his thumb,
And they all go marching down
Into ground to get out of the rain,
Boom! Boom! Boom!

(Repeat with the following words for each verse.)

Two...tie his shoe...
Three... climb a tree...
Four...shut the door...
Five...take a dive...
Six...pick up sticks...
Seven...pray to heaven...
Eight...shut the gate...
Nine...check the time...
Ten...say "THE END"
(Birkenshaw-Fleming, 1989, p. 170)

2. Adapt songs to highlight sounds, as in "Frere Jacques" (translated) "Are you sleeping?":

Are you sleeping?
Are you sleeping?
Brother John, Brother John?
Morning bells are ringing
Morning bells are ringing
Ding ding dong!
Ding ding dong!
(Ping ping pong)
(Ring rang rong)

An adaptation of "Three Little Monkeys" could be:

Five fine fish flopping on the bed.
One fell off and bumped his head!
Mama called the doctor. The doctor said,
No more fish flopping on the bed.

Activities Using Drama

1. Have children act out their favorite nursery rhyme and have their classmates try to guess the rhyme.

2. Mime a word that rhymes with a given word. The mimed word could be whispered to the student or it could be depicted on a card; for example, *ride/hide*.

Activities Using Art

1. Create a collage with pictures of favorite rhymes.

2. Have children make cards for a game of Snap. Children use a pack of cards that contain 10 pairs of rhyming words. The cards are shuffled, and each child plays a card. The child who shouts "snap" first when a pair of cards rhyme wins the cards.

3. Draw a picture of something that rhymes with the word *me*. A child may draw a tree, a bee, a key, etc.

4. Make a collection of objects that rhyme. Use pictures from magazines or real objects.

Activities Using Stories and Writing

1. Make up a shared story in small groups of four or five children. The story should include rhyming words.

2. Have children make up funny names for the characters in their favorite books, or for things that they saw on a field trip (for example, Baboo at the zoo).

3. Choose a reading selection loaded heavily with pairs of rhyming words. Then use peelable sticky notes to cover one of the rhyming pair so the children can predict the word. *Tog the Dog* (Hawkins & Hawkins, 1986) and *Lions and Gorillas* (Nelson, 1989) are good choices.

4. Read stories with many examples of alliteration. For example, use the alphabet book, *Animalia*, (Base, 1988); *The Teeny Tiny Woman* (O'Conner & Alley, 1986); or *Prairie Alphabet* (Banatyne-Cugnet & Moore, 1992).

5. Read rhyming texts to children each day. From repeated readings of rhyming and playful texts, children can develop a resource of passages that they can use as models for creating their own rhymes. For example, *The Itsy Bitsy Spider* (Traponi, 1993) might become "The Itsy Bitsy Ladybug."

6. Encourage daily writing experiences that give children practice trying to map spoken language into written language. The more experience they have with letters and sounds, the greater their understanding that words can be segmented into sounds (Griffith, Klesius, & Kromrey, 1992).

Conclusion

By engaging in enjoyable activities involving rhyme, alliteration, and sound judgement, children begin to analyze individual sounds in words.

About the Parent Letter and Lesson Plan

As in the previous chapter, this parent letter is to encourage parents to share rhymes with their children in preparation for a Nursery Rhyme Day at school.

The following lesson plan can be used to further develop children's phonological awareness of sound judgment, alliteration, and rhyming.

Parent Letter

Dear Family,

Awareness of sounds in words is very important in helping your child learn to read and write. Here are some activities you can do at home to increase your child's sound awareness:

- Sing "The Alphabet Song" with your child. (A, B, C, D....Z, now I know my A, B, Cs, next time won't you sing with me").
- Read books to your child. Talk about words that rhyme like *cat* and *hat*, and *mouse* and *house*. For example, you could say "Did you hear all those words that rhymed?" or "*Can* and *man*—those two words rhyme!" Talk about long words like *hippopotamus* or short words such as *I*. Talk about words and phrases that are fun to say: *Peter Piper picked a peck of pickled peppers*.
- Help your child think of words that rhyme with his or her name, with friends names, or with other family members' names.
- Help your child find words that rhyme in books by Dr. Seuss or other rhyming stories.
- Recite familiar nursery rhymes with your child like "Jack and Jill," "Twinkle, Twinkle Little Star," "Mary Had a Little Lamb," "Little Miss Muffet," "Humpty Dumpty," "Baa-Baa Black Sheep," "Old Mother Hubbard," and "Hickory Dickory Dock."

Occasionally, have your child finish parts of the rhyme "Little Miss Muffet sat on a _____."

- Help your child memorize one of the following rhymes for a Nursery Rhyme Day when children can recite their rhymes in small groups for parents who wish to attend the special day.

Jack and Jill went up the hill,
to fetch a pail of water.
Jack fell down and broke his crown,
and Jill came tumbling after.

Twinkle, twinkle little star,
how I wonder what you are.
Up above the world so high,
like a diamond in the sky.
Twinkle, twinkle little star,
How I wonder what you are.

Mary had a little lamb,
little lamb, little lamb.
Mary had a little lamb,
whose fleece was white as snow.
And everywhere that Mary went
Mary went, Mary went,
everywhere that Mary went,
that lamb was sure to go.

Little Miss Muffet
Sat on a tuffet,
Eating her curds and whey;

(continued)

Parent Letter (continued)

There came a big spider,
who sat down beside her
And frightened Miss Muffet away.

Humpty Dumpty sat on a wall,
Humpty Dumpty had a great fall,
All the King's horses and
all the King's men
couldn't put Humpty
together again.

Baa-baa Black Sheep
have you any wool?
Yes sir, yes sir,
three bags full.
One for my master
and one for the dame
and one for the little boy
who lives down the lane.

Old Mother Hubbard
went to the cupboard
to get her poor dog a bone
but when she got there her cupboard was bare
and so her poor dog had none.

Hickory Dickory Dock,
the mouse ran up the clock.
The clock struck one
the mouse ran down
Hickory Dickory Dock.

Two little Blackbirds
sitting on a wall, One named Peter
and the other named Paul
Fly away Peter
Fly away Paul,
Come back Peter,
Come back Paul.

Sample Lesson Plan for October and November

1. Have students clap out the number of syllables in either their first name or their last name when their name is called in attendance.
2. Introduce the /l/ sound. Provide auditory, visual, and kinesthetic feedback on how to produce /l/.
3. Have children sing the song "Mary Had a Little Lamb."
4. Write this song in the Big Book of rhyming selections.
5. Have students identify the words that rhyme. Talk about why the words rhyme.

Chapter 6

Isolating and Categorizing Sounds

As children become more familiar with sound play through activities like those in Chapter 5, more structured tasks like categorizing and isolating sounds can be integrated into the curriculum.

Maclean et al. (1987) reported that children who have knowledge of and experience with rhymes have learned to some degree that words are composed of individual sound components. Bradley and Bryant (1985) found that phonological oddity tasks (*bat, be, book, fish*) and categorization activities significantly reduced the occurrence of reading problems in preschoolers who initially evidenced poor phonological awareness skills.

Wallach and Wallach (1976) defined the phonological awareness task of isolating phonemes as pronouncing a beginning, medial, or final sound in isolation from a given word. For example, an isolation task might ask the question "What is the first sound in *fish*?" Lewkowicz (1980) states that this is a useful task because learning to isolate the initial phoneme is the first step in phoneme segmentation. In addition, it is reportedly a realistic activity in which kindergarten children can engage (Lewkowicz, 1980). Zhurova (1963–1964, as cited in Lewkowicz, 1980) also found that 4-year-olds can isolate initial sounds if they are taught properly.

Isolating and Categorizing Phonemes

Games for isolating and categorizing phonemes can be divided into three levels of complexity: knowledge of beginning and ending sounds, recognition of sounds, and generation tasks involving isolation or categorization of sounds.

Knowledge of Beginning and Ending Sounds (Receptive)

Talk about phonemic features. For example, the teacher might say "*K-k-k-cake, k-k-k-car, k-k-k-cat.* What sounds do these words start with?"

Recognition of Sounds (Receptive)

1. Create or use a collage that highlights a particular speech sound or rhyming words. Have children identify objects that rhyme or begin with the same sound.

2. Foster categorization skills through phonological oddity tasks (that is, teach children to categorize or group pictures

Identifying objects that rhyme or begin with the same sound.

of real objects together on the basis of shared sounds. For example, *pen* could be grouped with *pop* and *pan*, because they all start with the same sound. Letters can be used to represent the shared sound(s) in the set of pictures.

3. Have children determine which word in a series of two to four words does not share the same beginning or final sound with the other words (for example, *hat, hen, hill, cat*) (Bradley & Bryant, 1983, 1985).

4. Talk about and look at examples of words that have parts that are the same or different (*skinny, tiny*). Have children choose words that are similar from three or four choices (*shiny, smelly, nose*). Then have children give examples of other words with similar parts (*y* ending like *jelly* and *many*, and *ing* endings).

Generation Tasks (Expressive)

1. Encourage children to create new words like *duckey* or *mousey.* Have children make up a sentence and say it or write it with as many words with *y* endings as possible.

2. Have children explain how they chose the word that did not belong during rhyme and phonological oddity tasks.

3. Engage students in tasks requiring isolation of initial or final sounds. What is the first sound in *fish*? What is the last sound in *dog*?

4. Give children a number of familiar objects and ask them to find one that starts with the *s* sound.

5. Design activities around the sound of the day. For example, if /s/ is the sound of the day, attendance could be taken by substituting the initial consonant of each student's name. For example, *David* could be said as *Savid, Mary* could be said as *Sary* (Yopp, 1992).

6. Generate words that begin or end with specified sounds. For beginning sounds, ask for a word that starts with /b/. Say the sound not the letter name, *buh* not *be*. For ending sounds, ask for a word that ends with *ing.*

ISOLATING AND CATEGORIZING SOUNDS   **47**

Writing words ending with ing.

An Activity Using Nursery Rhymes and Other Rhymes

Select a rhyme that will match the sound of the day or week. If /m/ is the sound of the week, use a selection from *The Animated Alphabet™* (Stone, 1995).

An Activity Using Songs

Adapt the lyrics to familiar songs or melodies. For example, "Ring Around the Rosy" could be modified to "Ping around the posy" or "Ding around the dosy." The song "Three Blind Mice" can be used to highlight the relation between letters and sounds:

Buh buh buh, Buh buh buh;
Hear how it sounds, hear how it sounds.
It starts with /b/ and it sounds like this:

Buh, buh, buh, buh, buh, buh.
Kuh kuh kuh, Kuh kuh kuh;
Hear how it sounds, hear how it sounds.
It starts with /k/ and it sounds like this:
Kuh kuh kuh, kuh kuh kuh.

Different letters and their corresponding sounds can be substituted in the lyrics of the song. Songs are often repetitive and rhythmic in nature and, consequently, provide an excellent vehicle for children to explore sounds.

An adaptation of the words to the tune of "Head and Shoulders, Knees and Toes" is used to emphasize letters, sounds, and words beginning with similar sounds:

> *B* is the letter that sounds like *buh*,
> sounds like *buh*, sounds like *buh*,
> *B* is the letter that sounds like *buh*,
> in words like *ball*, *bat*, and *bee*!

Other words could be substituted (*bay*, *bite*, and *bye*) or alternate letters and sounds could be incorporated:

> /*K*/ is the letter that sounds like *kuh*,
> sounds like *kuh*, sounds like *kuh*,
> /*K*/ is the letter that sounds like *kuh*,
> in words like *key*, *cat*, and *car*!

The lyrics of "London Bridge" can also be easily adapted:

> /b/ is a sound that starts these words
> *ball*, *bounce*, *bear*, *ball*, *bounce*, *bear*
> /b/ is the sound that starts these words
> *ball*, *bounce*, *bear* and *b*_____
> (Goncalves et al., 1997).

Yopp (1992, pp. 699–700) provides a song that can be sung in the classroom to encourage children to generate words with specified sounds. To the tune of "Jimmy Cracked Corn," the following lyrics could be sung:

> Who has a /d/ word to share with us?
> Who has a /d/ word to share with us?

It must start with the /d/ sound!
(Each child's contribution can be incorporated)
Dog is a word that starts with /d/
Dog is a word that starts with /d/
Dog is a word that starts with /d/
Dog starts with the /d/ sound.

Melodies such as "Old MacDonald Had A Farm" also can be used with modified lyrics to facilitate knowledge of beginning and ending sounds (Yopp, 1992, pp. 699–700).

What's the sound that starts these words:
turtle, *time*, and *teeth*? (wait for a response)
/t/ is the sound that starts these words:
turtle, *time*, and *teeth*.
With a /t//t/ here, and a /t//t/ there,
here a /t/, there a /t/, everywhere a /t//t/.
/t/ is the sound that starts these words:
turtle, *time*, and *teeth*.

Change the sounds and words as you continue, for example, /ch/, *chair, chin, chalk.* You also can reinforce knowledge of middle and ending sounds by asking What is the sound in the middle of these words? or What is the sound at the end of these words?

The following are examples for focusing on the medial and final sounds:

What is the sound in the middle of these words:
leaf, and *deep*, and *meat*? (wait for a response)
/ee/ is the sound in the middle of these words:
leaf, and *deep*, and *meat.*
With an /ee/ /ee/ here, and an /ee/ /ee/ there,
Here an /ee/, there an /ee/, everywhere an /ee/ /ee/.
/ee/ is the sound in the middle of these words:
leaf, and *deep*, and *meat*!
What is the sound at the end of these words:
duck, and *coke*, and *beak*? (wait for a response)
/k/ is the sound at the end of these words:
duck, and *coke*, and *beak.*
With a /k//k/ here and a /k//k/ there

Here a /k/, there a /k/, everywhere a /k//k/.
/k/ is the sound at the end of these words:
duck, and *coke*, and *beak*!

See Appendix 1 for additional examples of word adaptations of songs.

Activities Using Drama

1. While sitting in a circle, have children take turns miming a verb that begins with a specific sound.
2. Draw the children's attention to the fun sound in words in a shared reading session by having the children chorally read predictable sections from *We're Going on a Bear Hunt* (Rosen & Oxenburg, 1989).

Activities Using Art

1. Use a patterned book, for example *Brown Bear, Brown Bear* (Martin & Carle, 1992), and invite the children to extend the text and paint illustrations.
2. Create a real or imaginary animal whose name starts with a particular letter.

Activities Using Stories and Writing

1. Read a text with rhyming throughout and ask the children to clap when they hear a rhyme (for example, *The Jolly Postman or Other People's Letters* by Ahlberg and Ahlberg, 1993).
2. Have the children in groups and pairs compose a rhyming letter.

Conclusion

Activities involving isolating and categorizing sounds help children to develop their ability to segment the individual sounds in words.

About the Parent Letter and Lesson Plan

Send this letter to parents to encourage them to play games and use stories that will develop their children's awareness of sounds and letters.

This lesson plan can be used to further develop children's ability to focus on sounds and letters.

Parent Letter

Dear Family,

Read stories often and talk about the story. Have your child tell you the story. Encourage your child to write about the story or draw a picture. Praise any attempts to read or write.

Talk about the sounds in words. For example, "the boy bounced his ball," "boy, bounce, ball" all those words start with the same sound, "buh." Have your child guess what sound words begin or end with, for example, ask "What is the first sound in the word *fish*? What sound do you hear at the end of the word *hat*?"

Point out letters and have your child name them. Can you find the letter that sounds like *m*?

Play I Spy with letters and sounds in words. For example, say "I spy with my little eye, something that begins with the letter *p* or the sound *puh*."

Sample Lesson Plan for December, January, and February

1. Introduce the /m/ sound. Provide auditory, visual, and kinesthetic feedback on how to produce the sound.

2. Read or recite the weekly rhyme selection.

3. Assist students with writing in their journal three words that begin with the /m/ sound and three words that end with the /m/ sound. Catalogues can be available at the journal center to help children find words or pictures with the /m/ sound.

Blending and Segmenting Syllables and Sounds

*C*hildren who have had experience with sound play and isolating and categorizing sounds can benefit from the higher level phonological awareness activities of blending and segmenting syllables and phonemes.

Blending and segmenting speech sounds is related closely to early reading and writing development (Griffith & Olson, 1992; Yopp, 1988). Blending is the act of articulating the sounds of a word together in order as in spoken language; whereas segmenting is defined as the process of separating or isolating sounds in words (Yopp, 1988). Children who can blend and segment speech sounds have an awareness of speech sound units. This phonological awareness enables them to learn how alphabet letters correspond to the sounds in words.

Kamhi (1992) states that phoneme blending and segmenting is too difficult a task for many kindergarten children, so it should not be introduced to children under age 4.

Here are several strategies that can be used when teaching blending and segmenting:

- Begin instruction at the syllabic level (Catts, 1991a; Liberman et al., 1974).
- Model and have children use slow and exaggerated pronunciation of the syllable or phoneme, so they can attend to both the articulatory and auditory clues (Lewkowicz, 1980).

- Increase children's familiarity with isolated speech sounds (Venezky, 1976).
- Implement teaching at increasing levels of difficulty from the sentence level, to compound words, to words, to syllables, and finally to phonemes (Fox & Routh, 1976).

Although blending tasks are reportedly easier than segmenting tasks (Helfgott, 1974, as cited in Lewkowicz, 1980), studies have shown that teaching segmenting skills first significantly helps children blend sounds. Therefore, segmenting should be targeted first (Fox & Routh, 1976; Lewkowicz, 1980). Elkonin (1963, 1964, as cited in Blachman, 1989) stated that the only effective way to develop skill analysis at the mental level is through practice in oral segmentation.

This chapter contains ideas for teaching children to blend and segment syllables and speech sounds. Activities begin with blending and segmenting syllables, because syllables in words are much easier to identify and manipulate than are sounds. These syllable-level tasks can help children learn that words can be divided into component parts. Once children have become familiar with blending and segmenting syllables, similar activities can be used to teach the blending and segmenting of sounds. Segmentation activities can be considered in a hierarchical order of difficulty as follows:

Sentences

"I'm going to say a sentence and I want you to clap once for each word. *My dog is black.*"

Compound Words

"I'm going to say two words that have been put together to make one word and I want you to clap once for each little word like *cow-boy.*" (A list of compound words can be found in Appendix 1.)

Syllables

"I'm going to say a word, and I want you to clap once for each part of a word or syllable." Say *el-e-phant*, then say it again as you clap out each syllable in the word.

Listening for Phonemes
    "I'm going to say a word, and I want you to clap once for each sound in the word *n–o*" (2 claps).

Recognizing Initial Phonemes
    "Whose name am I saying *M–ark or S–andy*?"

Isolating Phonemes
    "What are the three sounds in *fish*?"

Teaching Segmentation

   Segmentation is a phonological awareness skill in which children segment words into individual sounds. For example, *cat* when segmented becomes c-a-t.

Activities

   1. Letter-sound activities should be combined. Use magnetic letters and a magnet board.
   2. Introduce the sound of the day or week by having the children listen to the initial consonant exaggerated in a number of different examples. (See Chapter 8 for ways to highlight continuants and stops and also refer to Lindamood and Lindamood (1969) for an oral motor kinesthetic approach to teaching sounds.)
   3. Teach children to associate each sound with a picture. /S/ could be the snake sound; /l/ could be the singing sound "la la la."
   4. Remove segments from a sentence or word (*butterfly–butter–but*) (Fox & Routh, 1976).
   5. Have the children complete counting tasks in which they practice tapping the syllables and eventually phonemes of words. Decorate special tapping wands for this activity. Start by using compound words like *cowboy* or *pancake* and gradually introduce words like *baby* or *candy*. Next count the number of phonemes (sounds) in words. How many sounds can you tap in the word *fish*? (Clapping can be used instead of tapping wands.)

6. Teach children to segment spoken syllables into an initial consonant and the remaining portion of the word. That is, segment consonant–vowel (C:V) words (*n–o*), vowel–consonant (V:C) words (*i–t*), and then move to consonant–vowel-consonant (C:VC) words (*s–it*) in which the three-phoneme word is identical with the two-phoneme word except for the added consonant (*bee, beet; ape, tape*). Next, segment all the phonemes in a three-phoneme word (C:V:C words like *s-i-t*). Have children repeat the syllable as you pronounce it. Repeat the syllable with the designated sound deleted while you point to the letter magnets.

7. Use objects like disks, pennies, or tokens to represent the sounds of the word. This helps children monitor whether the number of sounds that they isolate match the number that they are supposed to have represented (Elkonin, 1963, 1964, as cited in Lewkowicz, 1980).

8. Use the "say it and move it" activity (adapted from Elkonin, 1963, 1973, as cited in Ball & Blachman, 1991). During this activity, children are taught to represent the sounds in one-,

Using pennies to represent the sounds in a word.

CHAPTER 7

two-, three-, and four-phoneme words by using manipulatives such as pennies or disks. The teacher can use a laminated sheet of paper with a picture of a basket or other object in the top half of the sheet and an arrow pointing from left to right on the bottom half of the sheet. A thick black line separates the top and bottom half of the sheet. The picture of the basket is used to store the pennies. The arrow is used to cue left-to-right movement. Following a model, the children can be taught to represent one sound (/p/) by one penny as they move the penny down to the arrow. Next, they can be taught to represent two sounds in a sequence (/b//g/). Once the students have learned to represent two sounds, two-, three-, and four-phoneme words can be introduced. The students are taught to say each word slowly as they use the pennies to represent each sound. Different colored chips can be used to represent vowels and consonants. Once children have developed knowledge of the alphabet and have some letter-sound correspondence, then objects can be used that have letters of the alphabet on them.

9. Another way to visually represent the phonemes in words is through the use of a series of connected boxes. Each box represents a sound (not the letters) in a word. For example, the word *cat* would be represented by three boxes joined horizontally (Elkonin, 1973, as cited in Lewkowicz, 1980).

10. Isolate the initial phoneme of the word in two ways: (1) by prolonging or stretching the initial sound while pronouncing the word and by varying your vocal loudness if it is a continuant, (*s, sh, th, f, v*); or (2) by repeating the initial sound two or three times before pronouncing the entire word (*p-p-p-p-pumpkin*) (the iteration method described by Zhurova, 1963, 1964, as cited in Lewkowicz, 1980) if it is a stop (*p, b, t, d, k, g*). Iteration can be used to exaggerate words in popular songs like "Pop Goes the Weasel." ("P-p-p-p-pop goes the weasel") (Yopp, 1992). It also can be used during an activity like attendance (initial consonants of children's names can be exaggerated using iteration, for example *L-L-L-L-Lisa.*)

11. Practice decoding some of the words that children have been able to segment.

Matching letters to sounds heard.

12. Adapt songs such as "Twinkle, Twinkle Little Star" by changing the words:

> Listen to the sounds you hear
> C-a-t. That spells cat.
> Listen to the sounds you hear
> D-o-g. That spells dog.

Teaching Blending

Blending is a phonological awareness skill in which children combine individual sounds to form words. For example, *b-a-t* when blended becomes *bat.*

Activities Using Games

1. Blend or articulate together isolated syllables to form multisyllabic words (Catts, 1991a). Start with compound words like *railroad* before trying words like *baby* in which the syllables do not have a referent. For example, go around a circle

of children and have them tell you what two words say when they are combined.

2. Divide compound words into syllables on flashcards (for example, *cow* and *boy*). Show the children each card separately. Next, say the syllable that corresponds to each card. Have the children take turns moving the cards together to make words (*cowboy*). As one child moves the card pieces together, the rest of the group can blend together the syllables and say the whole word.

3. Do an activity for sounds similar to that in No. 2. Say "I'm going to say some sounds and I want you to tell me what word they make. Listen: *p–an, p–an*. What word does *p–an* say?"

4. Work with C:V and V:C then two-part segmentation of CVC words: C:VC and CV:C then C:V:C segmentation. To ease the transition from CV and VC pairs, Lewkowicz (1980) recommends starting "with CV, CVC or VC, CVC pairs, in which the three-phoneme word is identical with the two-phoneme word except for the added consonant (e.g., *bee, beet; ape, tape*)" (p. 696, italics added).

The book *Sounds Abound* (Catts & Vartiainen, 1993) has pictures that can be used to help children learn to blend syllables and sounds.

5. Play a guessing game. Tell the class that you are thinking of an animal or a thing (a category name can be given that may correspond to a current unit or instructional theme). For example, the teacher might say, "I'm thinking of something that we have in our pond. It's a f-i-sh." The teacher says f-i-sh, articulating each sound separately. The students have to blend together the sounds to guess what the teacher is thinking of. The teacher might also want to extend a literacy experience. For example, "this is a character from today's story; it is a t-r-o-l-l."

6. Play a game with objects in a bag. Select one and say "I see a fea-ther." The student who guesses the object gets to hold the feather. All students in the group get a turn.

7. Play a game called "Fix it" described by Blachman (1989). In this activity a puppet with a moveable mouth tells segmented words to the class. For example, the puppet might

say b-a-g and the children have to fix it. Words can be embedded in sentences or short stories as well.

8. Use picture puzzles. Choose pictures and cut them into the number of syllables or sounds in a word.) Have the child say each syllable or sound after a model, then blend together the syllables or sounds to make the word as they put the puzzle together (Catts & Vartiainen, 1993). Use picture puzzles representing two-syllable words to introduce these skills. For example, cut a picture of a carrot into two pieces and then ask the children to say each syllable while they point to each part of the picture (segmenting) and then blend the syllables as they put together the puzzle (blending). This procedure also can be used to introduce sound segmentation and blending. Cut a picture of a cat into three pieces and have the students practice segmenting and blending the sounds in *c-a-t* as they put the puzzle together.

9. Give one child a secret picture. Have the child segment the word represented by the picture, and have the other children try to guess the picture by blending the phonemes that the segmenter produces. To make this easier, three or four pictures could be offered as choices for the segmenter and the blenders to choose from. As this task becomes easier for the blenders, the words represented by the pictures can become more phonologically similar.

An Activity Using Songs

Adapt songs as a blending activity. For example, adapt the song "Bingo."

> There was a teacher
> who had a student
> And Peter was his name
> P-e-t-e-r, P-e-t-e-r
> And Peter was his name.

At Christmas sing to the tune of "Bingo" the following Santa alphabet.

> There is a jolly, bearded man,
> And Santa is his name, Oh!

S-a-n-t-a, S-a-n-t-a, S-a-n-t-a,
and Santa is his name, Oh!

He's coming here on Christmas Eve,
And Santa is his name, Oh!
Clap-a-n-t-a, Clap-a-n-t-a, Clap-a-n-t-a,
And Santa is his name, Oh!

His sleigh is drawn by eight reindeer,
And Santa is his name, Oh!
Clap-Clap-n-t-a, Clap-Clap-n-t-a, Clap-Clap-n-t-a,

He slides down chimneys with his pack,
And Santa is his name, Oh!

He's dressed in red and brings us gifts,
And Santa is his name, Oh!

He'll come again another year,
And Santa is his name, Oh!
(Anonymous, in Birkenshaw-Fleming 1989, 137)

Activities Using Drama

1. Have children use their bodies to represent a letter.
2. Have three children make a word.
3. Have two children mime parts of a compound word.

An Activity Using Art

Write and illustrate a class alphabet book.

Activities Using Stories and Writing

Use key words in books to illustrate blending.

1. For example, in the story *Brown Bear, Brown Bear* (Martin & Carle, 1992), the green f-r-o-g sees a pruple c-a-t. Using the story *The Very Hungry Caterpillar* (Carle, 1974), children could be given tasks to segment or blend words in the story like the many fruits, vegetables, or meats that the caterpillar eats.

2. Read a story aloud to the children. As you read the story, segment words into their component syllables or sounds. Have the children put the words together (Blachman, 1991).

Write and illustrate a class alphabet book.

Conclusion

Phoneme blending and segmenting may be difficult for children who have not had experience with rhyming and isolating sound activities. These students will require more experience with rhyming and sound play before engaging in segmenting and blending activities.

About the Parent Letter and Lesson Plan

Send this letter to parents to encourage them to engage in interactive storytelling and sound play in their everyday conversations with their children.

The following lesson plan uses activities involving syllables and sounds to further develop phonological awareness.

Parent Letter

Dear Family,

By reading stories and talking about words and sounds in print, you are helping your child learn to read.

Read to and with your child everyday. Enjoy the chance to talk and share ideas about stories, words, and sounds.

Together write or draw pictures about stories.

Occasionally, play with sounds by exaggerating them or repeating them. For example, "I'm sssssssso tired. I want to gggggooooo to b-e-d." This activity works particularly well with familiar phrases or words.

Have your child find three objects in the house that begin with a specific sound.

Sample Lesson Plan for March, April, May, and June

1. Introduce the sound *buh*, which is the letter *b*.

2. Have students say their names with /b/ substituted for the initial consonant in their name when attendance is taken. *Martin* would say his name *Bartin*, and *Ruth* would say her name as *Buth*.

3. Sing the daily rhyme selection in your Big Book of rhyming selections: "Baa-Baa Black Sheep."

4. Use the "Say it and Move it" activity (adapted from Elkonin, 1963, 1973, as cited in Ball & Blachman, 1991) to segment the two-phoneme syllable /baa/. Also segment the following syllables into three units: *bat, ball, bit, bun,* and *bet*. (See Chapter 8 for a more detailed description of this activity.)

Letters and Sounds

Numerous studies have shown that phonological aware-ness teaching programs that include letter-name and letter-sound correspondence have a greater positive impact on reading development than interventions involving phonologi-cal awareness or sound-letter instruction alone. The instruc-tional sequence listed in this chapter was designed from a review of these studies (Ball & Blachman, 1991; Bradley & Bryant, 1983, 1985; Hohn & Ehri, 1983; Lundberg et al., 1988).

In *The Role of Phonics in Reading Instruction* (International Reading Association, 1997), the following three key statements are made:

- The teaching of phonics is an important aspect of be-ginning reading instruction.
- Classroom teachers in the primary grades do value and do teach phonics as part of their reading programs.
- Phonics instruction, to be effective in promoting inde-pendence in reading, must be embedded in the con-text of a total reading/language arts program.

Although this chapter provides a general guide for com-bining letter-sound teaching with phonological awareness pro-gramming, this sequence is not meant as a substitute for a read-ing program, but as one component of a meaningful reading and language arts program. It recommends that children might com-plete one letter-name and one letter-sound activity during each phonological awareness lesson. Many of these activities have been described or alluded to in the previous chapters. Activities should be placed in a meaningful context of real reading and writing. Letter-sound relations often are taught spontaneously to meet a child's needs at a particular time; for example, during journal writing a child may ask for help with spelling.

This chapter is divided into two parts, A and B. Part A can be taught in conjunction with Chapter 4, Fun with Sounds, and Chapter 5, Rhyme Time. The focus of Part A is on increasing students' awareness of letter-sound association. At this point in the program, most children will have mastered several letter names and their corresponding sounds. Part B can be introduced along with Chapter 6, Isolating and Categorizing Syllables and Sounds, and Chapter 7, Blending and Segmenting Syllables and Sounds. The focus of Part B is on making and breaking words.

Part A: Learning About Letters and Sounds

The following sections provide activities to increase students' abilities with letters and sounds.

1. Have children sing "The Alphabet Song" in unison. Once they become familiar with this song, point to each letter as it is sung.

2. Gradually introduce the relation between letters and sounds. Draw attention to letters in different ways. For example, illustrate a picture of an *s*, look at the name tags of students with the /s/ sound in their names, find classroom centers that are described with an *s* in their title (snack center), or point out words in Big Books that have the /s/ sound in them. You can use a variety of techniques to highlight how to make sounds such as providing an auditory cue (prolonging a sound /sssss/, repeating a sound /p-p-p-p-p/, or varying your vocal loudness by saying a sound loudly or softly), associating the sound with something with which children are familiar (/s/ is the snake sound; /k/ is the coughing sound), showing children a visual cue (hold the letter symbol up to your mouth as you make the sound, show how a puppet makes the sound, or look in a mirror), or telling them

how the sound is made (put your teeth together and put your tongue behind your teeth). Lindamood and Lindamood (1969) have reported success using the Auditory Discrimination In-Depth Program to highlight sound properties by discussing the characteristics that can be seen, heard, and felt.

3. Introduce one or two of the following continuants and nasals per week: /f, s, sh, v, th, z, n, m/. Work with phonemes only at the beginning of words, because beginning sounds are usually more easily recognized and easier to produce than sounds at the ends of words (Zhurova, 1964, as cited in Lewkowicz, 1980; Cavoures, 1964, as cited in Marsh & Mineo, 1977).

An alternate approach to introducing letters and sounds may be to introduce consonants that can be easily combined with vowels to make numerous word combinations (/s, o, r, t, p/). For instance, Ball and Blachman's (1991) letter-name and letter-sound instruction in sound-symbol relations, which used only nine letters (*a, m, t, i, s, r, f, u,* and *b*), could be used to create a significant number of real consonant-vowel-consonant (CVC) words. Novel consonants were matched with individual learned consonants according to the features of production (*f*/*v, m*/*n, t*/*d, s*/*z, p*/*b*).

As expressed in the International Reading Association position statement, phonics instruction is best introduced when embedded in meaningful language activities such as language experience, Big Book sharing, and shared writing (Juliebö, 1991, 1995).

4. Introduce letter-sound associations for vowels.

5. Based on students' needs, gradually introduce the following stop consonants and glides: /p, b, l, t, k/. Emphasize the properties of the chosen stop consonant by repeating the sound several times in a row (*p-p-p-p-p-p-p-pit*).

Repeating sounds in this manner is the reiteration method proposed by Zhuruva (1973), as cited in Lie (1991).

Summary of the Letter-to-Sound Correspondence

Letter Symbol	Examples	Letter Symbol	Example
p	as in pat	s	as in vision
b	as in bat	y	asin yellow

m	as in mat	w	as in water
n	as in no	h	as in hat
t	as in tea	d	as in dog
h	as in wheel	k	as in key
g	as in goat	ng	as in sing
f	as in fan	v	as in van
j	as in jet	sh	as in shoe
l	as in lamp	s	as in saw
z	as in zebra	r	as in read
ch	as in chair	th (voiceless)	as in thumb
th (voiced)	as in that		

Vowels	Examples	Vowels	Examples
a	as in bat	e	as in bed
i	as in bit	o	as in mop
u	as in up	a	as in cake
e	as in see	i	as in bike
o	as in smoke	u	as in cute
a	as in father	u	as in put

Letters that borrow the sounds of other letters	Examples
c	/k/ as in cat
c	/s/ as in city
x	/ks/ as in box
x	/z/ as in xylophone
qu	/kw/ as in queen
y	short i as in gym
y	long i as in my
e	short e as in yes
g	soft g as in ginger

Vacca, Vacca, and Gove (1991) claim that having children recognize larger groups of letters (that is, phonograms) is more effective than single-letter processing. Pool (1997) recommends the following phonograms for Grade 1 children:

Short–vowel phonograms

at	an	ap	and	ack	ash		
et	est	ell					
it	in	ip	ick	ing	ink	ill	
ot	op	ock					
ug	uck	ump	unk				

Long–vowel phonograms

ate	ake	ame	ale	ay	ain	ail
eat						
ide	ice	ine	ight			
oke	ore					

Alternate–vowel sounds

all	aw	ir	or

6. When introducing new letters and their corresponding sounds, highlight both the letters and the auditory sound representation.

7. Have children repeat the name of the letter and tell you the sound that the letter makes. Show them the letter and ask, "What sound does this letter make?" Children can be taught key words to help them remember the sound of each letter. (See Lindamood & Lindamood, 1969; Stone, 1995).

8. Practice matching the letters with the alphabet name (for example, "Show me the letter *b*").

9. Glue each letter of the alphabet, as well as a picture associated with the sound, onto 3" × 5" recipe cards. For example, glue on the letter S along with a picture of a snake and write a sentence full of s words.

10. Play games like Memory, Go Fish, Feed the Clown, and board games to increase children's familiarity with sounds. (See activities in this chapter for descriptions and ideas for sound games.) Stone's (1995) program also provides numerous ways to stimulate sound awareness.

11. Give the children practice naming the letters corresponding to the sounds. Make the sound of the letter, then have the child print the letter on a blank sheet of paper. Do this in activities such as language experience, shared writing, and making and breaking words (Cunningham & Cunningham, 1992).

Part B: Making and Breaking Words

Although many children develop spelling ability through invented spellings, some at-risk children need more specific teaching of letter-sound and sound-letter correspondence

(Adams, 1990; Clay, 1991). In Reading Recovery, Clay (1993) describes three techniques for guided invented spelling activities. These are Elkonin, magnetic letters, and story writing in which listening for sounds guide spellings (Clay, 1985).

Clay (1993) describes the Elkonin processes whereby children first match sounds they learn by moving counters (coins). For example the word *cat* would be represented by three counters. When the teacher is satisfied that the child can hear the sounds, letters are then introduced to mark the sounds. These letters are written into boxes by the teacher.

c	a	t	

The procedure begins with regular CVC words and moves to complex words such as *hamster* or *drummer*. For a detailed description of this technique, see *An Observation Survey of Early Literary Achievement* (Clay 1993).

Magnetic letters or cut-out letters can be used most successfully to show children how words can be made and

Moving counters into boxes that represent phonemes.

changed. For example, if the child knows the word *dad*, this can be changed to *had*, *sad*, *mad*, *man*, and *men*.

Cunningham and Hall (1994) developed an activity called "making words." In this process children are given a number of letters that they use to make a variety of words. These words are used to focus the children's attention on patterns in words. For example, words are sorted according to features such as rhyme, endings, beginning sounds, and plurals.

Activities for Developing Letter-Sound Awareness

Activities Using Games

1. Use flash cards and games like "Bingo" that require matching the words on the game board with a spoken word or picture.

2. Make a sound collage of objects whose names begin with *b*.

3. Play Go Fish. Create pairs of cards with matching words (two cards of *fish*, *forks*, *fans*, *lights*, *lambs*, and *lions*.) Shuffle the cards. Give each player three cards and place the rest of the cards face down on the table. Players take turns asking other players for cards that match the cards that they are holding. ("Do you have a word that starts with *f*?") If the opposing player does not have the matching card, he says "Go fish."

4. Play Feed the Clown. Place cards (with words and pictures representing a particular sound) face down. Children take turns selecting a card, naming the letter, telling what sound the word starts with, and feeding the card to the clown. (You can feed the cards to a puppet, or you can put sound-letter cards onto cookie shapes and feed them to a cookie monster.)

5. Play Memory. Have pairs of cards made up with the same words on them. Take turns turning over two cards at a time to see if they match. As you turn over a card, say the beginning sound of the word. For example, "This word begins with the letter *s* (say the name); it makes the sound /sssss/ (say the sound)."

6. Play board games. Children have to say a word that starts with the letter that you say before they can take their turn.

7. Play a flashlight game. Tack word cards to a wall. Have children sit facing the wall. Shut off the lights. Take turns shining the flashlight on cards and saying words' beginning letters and associated sounds.

An Activity Using Rhymes and Poems

Choose a rhyme to highlight a particular sound. For example, /k/; work with the rhymes the "Cat and the Fiddle" and "Hickory Dickory Dock."

Activities Using Songs

Adapt songs to focus on sounds and letters. To the tune of "Here We Go Round the Mulberry Bush," sing the following:

> Listen for the /k/ sound,
> the /k/ sound, the /k/ sound.
> Listen for the /k/ sound,
> in words like *key* and *cake*!

To the tune of "Old MacDonald Had A Farm" sing:

> Old MacDonald had some (*sugar, sheep, shoes*),
> ee-i-ee-i-oh
> With a *sh, sh* here,
> and a *sh, sh* there,
> ee-i-ee-i-oh.

Meintzer (1997) suggested an adaptation of the song "Where Oh Where Has My Little Dog Gone?"

> Where oh where has the letter *A* gone?
> Oh, where, oh where can it be?
> We need it for *apple*, a_____ and _____.
> Oh, where, oh where can it be?

This rhyme could be written on an erasable surface where the letter and words starting with the letter could be changed.

Hall (1991, as cited in Warren, 1991) describes an adapted song and activity for focusing on letter awareness (p. 78) sung to "The Paw Paw Patch."

> Picking up an *A* and put it in the basket,
> Picking up an *A* and put it in the basket,
> Picking up an *A* and put it in the basket,
> Way down yonder in the letter patch.

Write alphabet letters on index cards and place the cards on the floor. Put a basket in the middle of the floor. As you sing the song, have the children pick up cards with the letter *A* written on them and put them in the basket. Continue with other letters as desired.

(Appendix 1 provides additional reference materials for such activities.)

Activities Using Drama

1. Have children use their bodies to make letter shapes.

2. Have children mime a story read by the teacher (for example, parallel mime for *The Teeny Tiny Woman*, by O'Conner & Alley, 1996).

3. Take the children on a sound journey using a book. The journey is mapped by placing the sound words on flashcards or the chalkboard (for example, *On My Walk*, Framst & Halliday, 1991).

Activities Using Art

1. Draw a bee. Write the word bee. Make up a story about a bee.

2. Children go on a print walk and note all environmental signs in their notebooks.

3. Make spiders out of egg cartons when focusing on the *sp* blend. Attach spiders to a web made by the children.

Activities Using Stories and Writing

1. Have a wide variety of books available so that the children can read books independently (Juliebö, 1991). For an ex-

Children can write
and illustrate their
own alphabet books.

cellent guide to introducing a new book to a child see Clay
(b), (1991).

2. Highlight letters and sounds during the context of daily
activities (for example, *T* is for *Tom*; *superstore* has two /s/
sounds in it; how do you spell *Ann*? buh, buh, buh, b sound; what
word starts with *A*?; *P* is the sound for *pig* and *pet*; *Sam* and *sit*
both start with the sound /s/. What other words start with that
same sound?)

3. Use pictures with initial sound associations (for example, an apple and an ant for the letter *a*).

4. Encourage inventive spelling and teach good spelling
strategies (Tarasoff, 1990; Sitton, 1993).

5. Have children illustrate their own alphabet book.

Conclusion

Children who have developed phonological awareness
are able to understand and complete segmentation tasks with
phonemes. Phoneme segmentation is correlated strongly with
the ability to read. The highest level of awareness, phoneme

manipulation, requires that children add, delete, or move phonemes to generate new words. Phoneme manipulation is generally unattainable for children who have not received formal reading instruction (Adams, 1990), and researchers have commented that tasks requiring this level of phonological awareness are typically inappropriate for kindergarten age children. Adams (1990) comments that it is difficult to assess whether the skills required for phoneme manipulation tasks are causes or effects of reading.

Appendix 1

Helpful Lists, Materials, and Resources

This appendix includes the following information:
Sources for rhymes, songs, and poems.
Examples of song adaptations for sound awareness.
A list of phonograms (rhyming words).
A list of compound words.
Lists of one-, two-, three-, four-, five-, and six-syllable words;
Lists of sound blending words.
More resources for teaching phonological awareness.

Sources for Nursery Rhymes, Rhymes, Poems, and Songs

Anderson, P.F. (1995). *The Mother Goose pages.* Dreamhouse Nursery Bookcase. <http://pubweb.nwu.edu/~pfa/dream house/nursery/bookcase.html> (1998, February 1).

Anglund, J. W. (1960). *In a pumpkin shell.* (Alphabet Mother Goose). San Diego, CA: Harcourt Brace Jovanovich.

Anno, M. (1975). *Anno's alphabet.* New York: Crowell.

Aylesworth, J. (1992). *Old black fly.* (Stephen Gammell, Illus.). New York: Scholastic.

Azarian, M. (1981). *A farmer's alphabet.* Boston, MA: David Godine.

Baer, G. (1989). *Thump, thump, rat-a-tat-tat.* (Lois Ehlert, Illus.). New York: Harper & Row/Zolotow.

Barchas, S. E. (1975). *I was walking down the road.* (Jack Kent, Illus.). New York: Scholastic.

Base, G. (1986). *Animalia.* New York: Harry Abrams.

Baskin, L. (1972). *Hosie's alphabet.* New York: Viking Press.

Bayor, J. (1984). *A: My name is Alice.* (Steven Kellogg, Illus.) New York: Dial.

Benjamin, A. (1987). *Rat-a-tat, pitter pat.* (Margaret Miller, Photos). New York: Crowell.

Blake, Q. (1989). *Quinton Blake's ABC.* New York: Knopf.

Brown, M. W. (1993). *Four fur feet.* New York: Doubleday.

Browne, P. (1996). *A gaggle of geese: The collective names of the animal kingdom*. New York: Atheneum.

Buller, J., & Schade, S. (1988). *I love you, good night*. New York: Simon & Schuster.

Cameron, P. (1961). *"I can't," said the ant*. New York: Coward-McCan.

Carle, E. (1974). *All about Arthur (an absolutely absurd ape)*. New York: Franklin Watts.

Carlstrom, N. W. (1992). *Baby-O*. (Sucie Stevenson, Illus.). Boston, MA: Little, Brown.

Carter, D. (1990). *More bugs in boxes*. New York: Simon & Schuster.

Catalanotto, P. (1990). *Mr. Mumble*. New York: Orchard/Jackson.

Cherry, L. (1988). *Who is sick today?* New York: Dutton.

Chess, V. (1979). *Alfred's alphabet walk*. New York: Greenwillow.

DePaola, T. (1985). *Tomie DePaola's Mother Goose*. New York: Putnam.

de Regniers, B., Moore, E., White, M., & Carr, J. (1988). *Sing a song of popcorn*. New York: Scholastic.

Deming, A. G. (1994). *Who is tapping at my window?* New York: Penguin.

Ehlert, L. (1989). *Eating the alphabet: Fruits and vegetables from A to Z*. San Diego, CA: Harcourt Brace Jovanovich.

Emberley, B. (1992). *One wide river to cross*. Boston, MA: Little, Brown.

Enderle, J. R., & Tessler, S. G. (1996). *Nell Nugget and the cow caper*. (Paul Yalowitz Illus.). New York: Simon & Schuster.

Falls, C. B. (1923). *ABC book*. New York: Doubleday.

Fortunata. (1968). *Catch a little fox*. New York: Scholastic.

Framst, L. (1991). *On my walk*. (Betty Halliday, Illus.). Cecil Lake, BC: Louise Framst.

Galdone, P. (1968). *Henny Penny*. New York: Scholastic.

Geisert, A. (1986). *Pigs from A to Z*. Boston, MA: Houghton Mifflin.

Geraghty, P. (1992). *Stop that noise!* New York: Crown.

Greenaway, K. (1993). *A apple pie*. Lyon, MS: Derrydale.

Hague, K. (1984). *Alphabears: An ABC book*. (Michael Hague, Illus.). New York: Holt, Rinehart & Winston.

Hawkins, C., & Hawkins, J. (1986). *Tog the dog*. New York: G. P. Putnam's Sons.

Hilton, N. (1990). *Prince Lachlan*. (Ann James Illus.). New York: Orchard.

Hoffman, P. (1990). *We play*. (Sara Wilson, Illus.). New York: Scholastic.

Hutchins, P. (1972). *Good-night owl!* New York: Macmillan.

Hymes, L., & Hymes, J. (1964). *Oodles of noodles*. New York: Young Scott Books.

Knutson, K. *Ska-tat!* New York: Macmillan.

Kovalski, M. (1987). *The wheels on the bus*. Toronto, ON: Kids Can Press Ltd.

Krauss, R. (1985). *I can fly*. New York: Golden Press.

Kuskin, K. (1990). *Roar and more*. New York: HarperTrophy.

Lansky, B. (1993). *The new adventures of Mother Goose: Gentle rhymes for happy times.*(Stephen Carpenter, Illust.). Deerhaven, MN: Meadowbrook.

Lee, D. (1974). *Nicholas Knog and other people*. (Frank Newfeld, Illus.). Toronto, ON: Macmillan.

Lee, D. (1977). *Garbage*. (Frank Newfeld, Illus.). Toronto, ON: Macmillan.

Lee, D. (1979). *Alligator pie*. (Frank Newfeld, Illus.) Toronto, ON: Macmillan.

Lee, D. (1983). *Jelly belly*. (Juan Wijngaard, Illus.). Toronto, ON: Macmillan.

Lewison, W. (1992). *Buzz said the bee*. New York: Scholastic.

Linscott, J. (1991). *Once upon A to Z: An alphabet odyssey*. (Claudia Porges Holland, Illus.). New York: Doubleday.

Martin, B. (1974). *Sounds of a powwow*. New York: Holt, Rinehart, & Winston.

Martin, B., Jr., & Archambault, J. (1989). *Chicka chicka boom boom*. (Lois Ehlert, Illus.). New York: Simon & Schuster.

Marzollo, J. (1989). *The teddy bear book*. New York: Dial.

McLenighan, V. (1982). *Stop-go, fast-slow*. Chicago, IL: Children's Press.

McPhail, D. (1989). *David McPhail's animals A to Z*. New York: Scholastic.

Musgrove, M. (1976). *Ashanti to Zulu: African traditions.* (Leo and Diane Dillon, Illus.). New York: Dial.

O'Connor, J. (1986). *The teeny tiny woman.* (R. W. Alley, Illus.) New York: Random House.

Obligado, L. (1983). *Faint frogs feeling feverish and other terrifically tantalizing tongue twisters.* New York: Viking.

Ochs, C. P. (1991). *Moose on the loose.* Minneapolis, MN: Carolrhoda Books.

Otto, C. (1991). *Dinosaur chase.* New York: HarperTrophy.

Owens, M. B. (1988). *A caribou alphabet.* Brunswick, ME: Dog Ear Press.

Pallotta, J. (1989). *The yucky reptile alphabet book.* (Ralph Masiello, Illus.). New York: Trumpet Club.

Parry, C. (1991). *Zoomerang-a-boomerang: Poems to make your belly laugh.* New York: Puffin Books.

Patience, J. (1993). *An amazing alphabet.* New York: Random House.

Patz, N. (1983). *Moses supposes his toeses are roses.* San Diego, CA: Harcourt Brace Jovanovich.

Pomerantz, C. (1993). *If I had a paka.* New York: Mulberry.

Prelutsky, J. (1982). *The baby Uggs are hatching.* New York: Mulberry.

Prelutsky, J. (1986). *Read-aloud rhymes for the very young.* (Marc Brown, Illus.) New York: Knopf.

Prelutsky, J. (1989). *Poems of A. nonny mouse.* New York: Alfred A. Knopf.

Provenson, A., & Provenson, M. (1977). *Old Mother Hubbard.* New York: Random House.

Raffi. (1987). *Down by the bay.* New York: Crown.

Raffi. (1989). *Tingalayo.* New York: Crown.

Rowell, P. (1996). *Just dessert.* San Diego, CA: Harcourt Brace.

Sendak, M. (1962). *Chicken soup with rice.* New York: Harper Collins.

Sendak, M. (1990). *Alligators all around: An alphabet.* New York: HarperTrophy.

Seuss, Dr. (1963). *Dr. Seuss's ABC.* New York: Random House.

Seuss, Dr. (1965). *Fox in socks.* New York, NY. Random House.

Seuss, Dr. (1974). *There's a wocket in my pocket*. New York: Random House.

Shaw, N. (1989). *Sheep on a ship*. Boston, MA: Houghton Mifflin.

Showers, P. (1991). *The listening walk*. New York: Harper Trophy.

Silverstein, S. (1964). *A giraffe and a half*. New York: Harper Collins.

Slepian, J., & Seidler, A. (1967). *The hungry thing*. (Richard E. Martin, Illus.). New York: Follet.

Staines, B. (1989). *All God's critters got a place in the choir*. New York: Penguin.

Sturges, P. (1996). *What's that sound, wolly bear?* (Joan Paley, Illus.). Boston, MA: Little, Brown.

Tajuri, N. (1983). *Early morning in the barn*. Middlesex, UK: Puffin/Penguin Books.

Tallon, R. (1979). *Zoophabets*. New York: Scholastic.

Thornhill, J. (1988). *The wildlife A-B-C: A nature alphabet book*. New York: Simon & Schuster.

Van Allsburg, C. *The Z was zapped*. Boston, MA: Houghton Mifflin.

Winthrop, E. (1986). *Shoes*. New York: HarperTrophy.

Wise Brown, M. (1947). *Goodnight moon*. (Clement Hurd, Illus.). New York: HarperCollins.

Yektai, N. (1987). *Bears in pairs*. New York: Macmillan.

Examples of Song Adaptations for Sound Awareness

Familiar songs can be used for playing with sounds. For example, the song "Twinkle, Twinkle, Little Star" can be substituted using "la, la, la, la" throughout. The "Happy Birthday" song can be sung by repeating a particular syllable such as "Baba baba baba" (Yopp, 1992).

Adaptations of familiar tunes:

Yopp (1992, p. 701) inserts sound play into the lyrics of "I've been working on the railroad":

I have a song that we can sing
I have a song that we can sing
I have a song that we can sing
It goes something like this:
Fe-Fi-Fiddly-i-o
Fe-Fi-Fiddly-i-ooooo
Fe-Fi-Fiddly-i-oooooo
Now try it with the /z/ sound!
Ze-Zi-Ziddly-i-o
Ze-Zi-Ziddly-i-oooooo
Ze-Zi-Ziddly-i-oooooo
Now try it with the /br/ sound!

Phonograms

Some of the easiest words for making up rhymes are:

cat, hat, bat, sat, mat, fat, gnat, and pat
well, shell, sell, tell, and bell
hide, ride, and slide
kite, white, might, night, sight, light, and fight
row, bow, no, snow, sew, low, go, and toe
fun, one, sun, done, bun, and run
pie, bye, cry, sigh, tie, why, my, high, and die
cake, flake, bake, snake, take, and lake
feet, meet, seat, beat, neat, and peat
bear, tear, dare, wear, pair, and fair
tea, bee, me, sea, three, and key
cow, how, now, vow, and meow

Bush (1989) provides an extensive list of phonograms. She also provides sentences that can be used in a rhyme generation task (*The little mouse went into the _____*).

See also *Sounds Abound* by Catts and Vartiainen (1993) for alternate activity sheets and lists and pictures of rhyme pairs. Lazzari & Peters (1989) have developed a handbook that includes worksheets on rhyming, isolating and combining sound, and segmenting and blending. Bradley (1988) recommends the formation of mother and child nursery rhyme groups.

The parent-child Mother Goose project (Heath Canada, 1995) was established to encourage mothers to use nursery rhymes as an entertaining and educationally beneficial way to bond with their children. It includes rhymes that focus on pairing movement and action with rhythmic passages.

Compound Words:

barnyard	batman	mainland	snowplow
blowout	carefree	newsstand	weekend
chairman	cowpoke	popcorn	surfboard
crossroad	downstream	sawmill	tomcat
fairground	foreword	scarecrow	trademark
hallway	handcuff	seaport	uproot

Bush (1989) lists several pages of compound words in her book.

Lists of One-, Two-, Three-, Four-, Five-, and Six-Syllable Words

Bush (1989) has developed extensive lists of mono- and multisyllabic words.

One-Syllable Words:

add	dear	heat
ape	do	have
bat	feet	jog
bite	fit	judge
cat	go	king
cut	game	kick

Two-Syllable Words

apple	zebra	popcorn
cobra	candy	doctor
Easter	hockey	present
swimming	summer	winter

Three-Syllable Words

September	October	telephone
hospital	spaghetti	banana
photograph	cucumber	octopus
instrument	principal	Saturday

Four-Syllable Words:

Cinderella	television	rhinoceros
kindergarten	caterpillar	dictionary

Five-Syllable Words

congratulations	refrigerator

Six-Syllable Words

encyclopedia	veterinarian

APPENDIX 1

Sound Blending Words

Use lists of one-, two-, three-, four-, and five-phoneme words. Segment the sounds in words and have the children attempt to blend together the sounds (*g-a-me*). Bush (1989) provides lists of segmented multiphoneme words.

Bush (1989) also provides lists of categories with words representing each letter of the alphabet. For instance, under the category Transportation, she lists *ambulance* and *automobile* under *A* and *bicycle* and *bulldozer* under *B*.

More Resources for Teaching Phonological Awareness

Adams, M.J. (1990). *Beginning to read: Thinking and learning about print*. Cambridge, MA: MIT Press.
This book is an excellent resource for teaching reading decoding.

Birkenshaw-Fleming, L. (1989). *Come on everybody let's sing*. Toronto, ON: Gordon V. Thompson Music.
This book contains a wide variety of musical activities for regular, mainstream, and special education classes.

Bush, C. (1989). *Language remediation and expansion: 150 skill building reference lists*. Tucson, AZ: Communication Skill Builders.
This book contains numerous lists of words and various sentence structures.

Catts, H., & Vartiainen, T. (1993). *Sounds abound*. East Moline, IL: Lingui Systems.
This is a great resource for worksheet activities on rhyming, isolating, and categorizing sounds, and on blending and segmenting sounds. It also references books and other resources that can be used to enhance knowledge of rhyme.

Fry, E., Fountoukidis, D.L., & Polk, J.K. (1985). *The new reading teacher's book of list*. Upper Saddle River, NJ: Prentice-Hall.
This book contains a variety of word lists for word identification and vocabulary activities.

Lazzari, A.M., & Peters, P.M. (1989). *Help 4: Handbook of exercises for language processing*. E. Moline: Lingui Systems.
This resource contains a number of useful worksheets to use in small groups of children or as parent handouts.

Lindamood, C., & Lindamood, P. (1969). *Auditory discrimination in depth*. Boston, MA: Teaching Resources.
This program is detailed and comprehensive. It has been widely adapted in classrooms, particularly with older students with reading difficulties (Grade 3).

Robertson, C., & Salter, W. (1997). *The phonological awareness test*. East Moline, IL: Lingui Systems.
This is a good tool for assessing phonological awareness.

Robertson, C., & Salter, W. (1995). *The phonological awareness kit*. East Moline, IL: Lingui Systems.
This kit consists of a manual of phonological awareness activities and a set of manipulatives.

Yopp, H. (1995b). Read-aloud books for developing phonemic awareness: An annotated bibliography. *The Reading Teacher, 48*(6), 538–543.
This article provides an excellent annotated bibliography of read-aloud books for developing phonological awareness.

Stone, J. (1995). *The Animated-Alphabet* (™). La Mesa, CA: J. Stone Creations.
This is part of Stone's program, The Animated-Literacy (™) Approach To Integrated Language Arts Instruction.

Schiller, P., & Moore, T. (1993). *Where is Thumbkin?* Mt. Rainier, MD: Gryphon House.
This is a collection of over 500 activities to use with well-known songs.

Appendix 2

Preteaching Test: Rhyme Detection

Teacher: Rhymes are words that sound the same at the end. *Bat* rhymes with *cat*; *man* rhymes with *can*. Does *ball* rhyme with *tall*? Yes, *ball* rhymes with *tall*. Not all words rhyme. Does *book* rhyme with *cup*? No, *book* and *cup* do not rhyme because *book* ends with *ook* and *cup* ends with *up*. Does *all* rhyme with *tall*? Yes! Now I am going to say some words, and I want you to tell me if they rhyme.

1.	dad–sad	11.	me–see
2.	set–get	12.	game–can
3.	head–bed	13.	want–went
4.	cook–bee	14.	joy–boy
5.	eat–seat	15.	moon–soon
6.	farm–car	16.	say–may
7.	been–seen	17.	snow–cold
8.	come–mom	18.	cake–make
9.	cow–bird	19.	store–more
10.	flower–power	20.	light–night

Score: ____/20
($x = 14$)

Children tested in April and May of the kindergarten year scored a mean of 14/20 on this task and it took approximately 1 to 2 minutes to administer (Yopp, 1988).

Appendix 3

Preteaching Test: Blending

Teacher: Try to guess what word I am saying. *C-ar*, what word did I say?

1. i–s	16. c–at
2. d–o	17. s–eat
3. b–e	18. st–ep
4. i–t	19. m–ine
5. m–y	20. s–it
6. t–o	21. d–o–g
7. o–n	22. b–a–g
8. s–ee	23. c–u–p
9. u–p	24. s–i–ck
10. i–n	25. b–oo–k
11. m–om	26. c–oa–t
12. c–ut	27. m–a–n
13. h–ead	28. f–i–ve
14. b–all	29. w–a–sh
15. l–eg	30. h–ea–t

Score: _____ /30
(x = 20)

Appendix 4

Preteaching Test: Segmenting

Teacher: I have a special language that I want to teach you. In this language, words are said in a special way. Words are broken apart and each sound is said separately. For example, the word *up* is said /u//p/. The word *dog* is said like /d//o//g/. The word *duck* is said like /d//u//k/. Now it is your turn to try. Say *seat*. Right /s//ea//t/. Now try these words:

1. is	12. no
2. cat	13. boy
3. men	14. sit
4. to	15. in
5. car	16. do
6. bee	17. leg
7. sun	18. on
8. if	19. cup
9. ball	20. yes
10. so	21. me
11. pen	22. won

Score: _____ /22

Yopp (1988) found that children in April and May of the kindergarten year achieved a mean score of 12 out of 22.

Appendix 5

Preteaching Test: Invented Spelling

The following words have been selected on the basis of high frequency in reading and writing of Kindergarten and Grade 1 children.

1.	the	I see the boy.	the
2.	big	This is a big apple.	big
3.	is	Here is a cat.	is
4.	it	Look at it.	it
5.	that	Is that your hat?	that
6.	he	Is he your brother?	he
7.	to	Go to the store.	to
8.	I	I like ice cream.	to
9.	in	Look in the box.	in
10.	was	The girl was here.	was
11.	are	These are red apples.	are
12.	his	Can you see his pencil?	his
13.	have	I have two sisters.	his
14.	not	I am not going home.	not
15.	with	Come with me.	with
16.	and	One and one are two.	and
17.	as	He is as big as you.	as
18.	they	Do they live here?	they
19.	of	This is a box of chocolates.	of
20.	a	This is a big story.	a

Stage 1	Stage 2	Stage 3	Stage 4

Appendix 6

Postteaching Test: Rhyme Detection

Teacher: Rhymes are words that sound the same at the end. *Bat* rhymes with *cat*; *man* rhymes with *can*. Does *ball* rhyme with *tall*? Yes, *ball* rhymes with *tall*. Not all words rhyme. Does *book* rhyme with *cup*? No, *book* and *cup* do not rhyme because *book* ends with *ook* and *cup* ends with *up*. Does *all* rhyme with *tall*? Yes! Now I am going to say some words, and I want you to tell me if they rhyme:

1. dad–sad	11. me–see
2. set–get	12. game–can
3. head–bed	13. want–went
4. cook–bee	14. joy–boy
5. eat–seat	15. moon–soon
6. farm–car	16. say–may
7. been–seen	17. snow–cold
8. come–mom	18. cake–make
9. cow–bird	19. store–more
10. flower–power	20. light–night

Score: _____ /20

Appendix 7

Postteaching Test: Blending

Teacher: Try to guess what word I am saying. *C-ar*, what word did I say?

1. i–s	16. c–at
2. d–o	17. s–eat
3. b–e	18. st–ep
4. i–t	19. m–ine
5. m–y	20. s–it
6. t–o	21. d–o–g
7. o–n	22. b–a–g
8. s–ee	23. c–u–p
9. u–p	24. s–i–ck
10. i–n	25. b–oo–k
11. m–om	26. c–oa–t
12. c–ut	27. m–a–n
13. h–ead	28. f–i–ve
14. b–all	29. w–a–sh
15. l–eg	30. h–ea–t

Score: _____ /30
(x = 20)

This task was an adaptation of a test described in Yopp (1988) called the Roswell–Chall Test of Auditory Blending (1959, as cited in Yopp, 1988).

Appendix 8

Postteaching Test: Segmenting

Teacher: I have a special language that I want to teach you. In this language, words are said in a special way. Words are broken apart and each sound is said separately. For example, the word *up* is said /u//p/. The word *dog* is said like /d//o//g/. The word *duck* is said like /d//u//k/. Now it is your turn to try. Say *seat*. Right /s//ea//t/. Now try these words:

1. is	12. no
2. cat	13. boy
3. men	14. sit
4. to	15. in
5. car	16. do
6. bee	17. leg
7. sun	18. on
8. if	19. cup
9. ball	20. yes
10. so	21. me
11. pen	22. won

Score: _____ /22

Appendix 9

Postteaching Test: Invented Spelling

The following words have been selected on the basis of high frequency in reading and writing of Kindergarten and Grade 1 children.

1.	the	I see the boy.	the
2.	big	This is a big apple.	big
3.	is	Here is a cat.	is
4.	it	Look at it.	it
5.	that	Is that your hat?	that
6.	he	Is he your brother?	he
7.	to	Go to the store.	to
8.	I	I like ice cream.	to
9.	in	Look in the box.	in
10.	was	The girl was here.	was
11.	are	These are red apples.	are
12.	his	Can you see his pencil?	his
13.	have	I have two sisters.	his
14.	not	I am not going home.	not
15.	with	Come with me.	with
16.	and	One and one are two.	and
17.	as	He is as big as you.	as
18.	they	Do they live here?	they
19.	of	This is a box of chocolates.	of
20.	a	This is a big story.	a

Stage 1	Stage 2	Stage 3	Stage 4

Adams, M.J. (1990). *Beginning to read: Thinking and learning about print.* Cambridge, MA: Massachusetts Institute of Technology Press.

Alberta Education. (1997). *Western Canadian protocol—English language arts.* Edmonton, AB: Author.

Ball, E. (1993). Assessing phoneme awareness. *Language, Speech, and Hearing in Schools, 24,* 130–139.

Ball, E., & Blachman, B.A. (1991). Does phoneme awareness training in kindergarten make a difference in early word recognition and developmental spelling? *Reading Research Quarterly, 26,* 49–66.

Blachman, B.A. (1989). Phonological awareness and word recognition: Assessment and intervention. In A. Kamhi & H. Catts (Eds.), *Reading disabilities: A developmental language perspective,* pp. 138–158. Needham Heights, MA: Allyn & Bacon.

Blachman, B.A. (1991). Early intervention for children's reading problems: Clinical applications of the research in phonological awareness. *Topics in Language Disorders, 12,* 51–65.

Bradley, L. (1988). Rhyme recognition and reading and spelling in young children. In R.L. Masland & M.W. Masland (Eds.), *Preschool prevention of reading failure.* Parkton, MD: York Press.

Bradley, L., & Bryant, P. (1983). Categorizing sounds and learning to read: A causal connection. *Nature, 271,* 746–747.

Bradley, L., & Bryant, P. (1985). *Rhyme and reason in reading and spelling.* Ann Arbor, MI: University of Michigan Press.

Bush, C. (1989). *Language remediation and expansion: 150 skill building reference lists.* Tucson, AZ: Communication Skill Builders.

Calfee, R., Chapman, R., & Venezky, R. (1972). How a child needs to think to learn to read. In L. Gregg. (Ed.), *Cognition in learning and memory* (pp. 139–182). New York: Wiley.

Catts, H.W. (1989). Phonological processing deficits and reading disabilities. In A. Kamhi & H.W. Catts (Eds.), *Reading disabilities: A developmental language perspective* (pp. 101–132). Austin, TX: Pro-Ed.

Catts, H.W. (1991a). Facilitating phonological awareness: Role of speech-language pathologists. *Language, Speech, and Hearing Services in Schools, 22,* 196–203.

Research References

Catts, H.W. (1991b). Early identification of reading disabilities. *Topics in Language Disorders, 12*(1), 1–16.

Catts, H.W. (1995). *Language basis of reading disabilities: Implications for early identification and remediation.* Paper presented at the annual conference of the Speech, Language, & Hearing Association of Alberta, Canada.

Catts, H.W., & Vartiainen, T. (1993). *Sounds abound: Listening, rhyming, and reading.* East Moline, IL: Lingui Systems.

Cavoures, G. (1964). *Phoneme identification in primary reading and spelling.* Unpublished doctoral dissertation, University of Boston, Massachusetts.

Clay, M.M. (1985). *The early detection of reading difficulties* (3rd ed.). Portsmouth, NH: Heinemann.

Clay, M.M. (1991). Introducing a new storybook to young readers. *The Reading Teacher, 45*(4), 264–272.

Clay, M.M. (1993). *An observation survey of early literacy achievement.* Portsmouth, NH: Heinemann.

Clay, M.M. (1991). *Becoming literate: The construction of inner control.* Portsmouth, NH: Heinemann.

Cunningham, P.M., & Cunningham, S.W. (1992). Making words: Enhancing the invented spelling-decoding connection. *The Reading Teacher, 46*, 106–115.

Cunningham, P., & Hall, D. (1994). *Making big words.* Parsippany, NJ: Good Apple.

Cunningham, P., & Hall, D. (1994). *Making words.* Parsippany, NJ: Good Apple.

Elkonin, D.B. (1973). Methods of teaching reading: USSR. In J. Downing (Ed.), *Comparative reading: Cross-national studies of behavior and processes in reading and writing* (pp. 551–578). New York: Macmillan.

Feuerstein, R., & Mentzker, Y. (1993). *Mediated learning experience (MLE): Guidelines for parents.* Hadazzah Wizo, Jerusalem, Israel: The Shulamit Iosupovici Institute for Community, Parental and Family Oriented Intervention.

Fox, B., & Routh, D.K. (1976). Phonemic analysis and synthesis as word attack skills. *Journal of Educational Psychology, 68*, 70–74.

Fox, B., & Routh, D.K. (1984). Phonemic analysis and synthesis as word attack skills: Revisited. *Journal of Educational Psychology, 76*, 1059–1061.

Fry, E.B., Fountoukidis, D.L., & Polk, J.K. (1985). *The new reading teacher's book of lists.* Upper Saddle River, NJ: Prentice-Hall.

Gillam, R.B., & van Kleeck, A. (1996). Phonological awareness training and short-term working memory: Clinical implications. *Language Disorders, 17*, 72–81.

Goncalves, M.L., Ericson, L., Gascoyne, C., & Juliebö, M.F. (1997). Phonological awareness: Suggestions for classroom teachers. *Early Childhood Education, 30*(1), 34–37.

Griffith, P., Klesius, J., & Kromrey, J. (1992). The effect of phonemic awareness on the literacy development of first grade children in a traditional or a whole language classroom. *Journal of Research in Childhood Education, 6*, 85–92.

Griffith, P., & Olson, M. (1992). Phonemic awareness helps beginning readers break the code. *The Reading Teacher, 45*, 516–523.

Helfgott, J.A. (1974). *Phoneme segmentation and blending skills of kindergarten children.* Unpublished doctoral dissertation, University of Connecticut.

Hodson, B.W. (1994). Foreword. *Topics in Language Disorders, 14*, vi.

Hohn, W., & Ehri, L. (1983). Do alphabet letters help prereaders acquire phonemic segmentation skill? *Journal of Educational Psychology, 75*, 752–762.

Health Canada. (1995). *Parents, kids, and Mother Goose: The parent-child Mother Goose program.* Edmonton, AB: Author.

International Reading Association. (1997) *The role of phonics in reading instruction.* A position statement of the International Reading Association. Newark, DE: Author.

Juel, C., Griffith, P., & Gough, P. (1986). Acquisition of literacy: A longitudinal study of children in first and second grade. *Journal of Educational Psychology, 78*, 243–255.

Juel, C. (1988). Learning to read and write: A longitudinal study of fifty-four children from first through fourth grade. *Journal of Educational Psychology, 80*, 437–447.

Juliebö, M.F. (1991). *Resource book for helping young children become readers.* Edmonton, AB: Reidmore.

Juliebö, M.F. (1995). Early literacy: Some continuing concerns. In L. Wason-Ellam, A. Blunt, & S. Robinson (Eds.), *Horizons of literacy, Part 2: Learning to be literate*, pp. 83–90. Winnipeg, MB: Hignell.

Kamhi, A. (1992). *Assessment and intervention of developmental language and reading disorders in school-age children.* Presented at the annual conference of the Speech, Language, and Hearing Association of Alberta, Canada.

Kamhi, A., & Catts, H.W. (1991). *Reading disabilities: A developmental language perspective.* Boston, MA: Allyn & Bacon.

Larsen, S.C., & Hammill, D.D. (1994). *Test of written spelling* (3rd ed.). Toronto, ON: Psycan.

Lazzari, A.M., & Peters, P.M. (1989). *Help 4: Handbook of exercises for language processing.* East Moline, IL: Lingui Systems.

Lewkowicz, N. (1980). Phonemic awareness training: What to teach and how to teach it. *Journal of Educational Psychology, 72,* 686–700.

Liberman, I.Y., Shankweiler, D., Fischer, F.W., & Carter, B. (1974). Explicit syllable and phoneme segmentation in the young child. *Journal of Experimental Child Psychology, 18,* 201–212.

Lie, A. (1991). Effects of a training program for stimulating skills in word analysis in first-grade children. *Reading Research Quarterly, 23,* 263–284.

Lindamood, C., & Lindamood, P. (1969). *Auditory discrimination in depth.* Boston, MA: Teaching Resources.

Lundberg, I., Frost, J., & Peterson, O. (1988). Effects of an extensive program for stimulating phonological awareness in preschool children. *Reading Research Quarterly, 23,* 263–284.

Lundberg, I., Olofsson, A., & Wall, S. (1980). Reading and spelling skills in the first school years, predicted from phonemic awareness skills in kindergarten. *Scandinavian Journal of Psychology, 21,* 59–173.

Maclean, M., Bryant, P., & Bradley, L. (1987). Rhymes, nursery rhymes, and reading in early childhood. *Merrill–Palmer Quarterly, 33,* 255–281.

Marsh, G., & Mineo, J. (1977). Training preschool children to recognize phonemes in words. *Journal of Educational Psychology, 69,* 748–753.

Meintzer, J. (1997). *Personal interview.* Edmonton, AB.

Nicholson, T. (1997). *Does phonemic awareness training improve the literacy skills of low–SES children?* Unpublished paper, University of Auckland, New Zealand.

Pool, J. (1997). *Early reading intervention.* Unpublished manuscript, Continuing Professional Education, University of Alberta, Canada.

Pratt, A.C., & Brady, S. (1988). Relation of phonological awareness to reading disability in children and adults. *Journal of Educational Psychology, 80,* 319–323.

Robertson, C., & Salter, W. (1995). *The phonological awareness profile.* East Moline, IL: Lingui Systems.

Rosner, J. (1971). *Phonic analysis training and reading skills* (Report No. RE-004-006). Pittsburgh, PA: University of Pittsburgh, Learning Research and Development Center. (ERIC Document Reproduction Service No. ED 059 029)

Roswell–Chall auditory blending test. (1959). New York: Essay Press.

Sawyer, D.J. (1988). Studies of the effects of teaching auditory segmenting skills within the program. In R. Masland & M. Masland (Eds.), *Preschool prevention of reading failure* (pp. 121–142). Parkton, MD: York Press.

Schuele, C.M., & van Kleeck, A. (1987). Precursors to literacy: Assessment and intervention. *Topics in Language Disorders, 7*(2), 32–44.

Share, D.L., Jorm, A.F., Maclean, R., & Matthews, R. (1984). Sources of individual differences in reading acquisition. *Journal of Experimental Psychology, 76,* 1309–1324.

Sitton, R. (1996). *Spelling sourcebook 1.* Spokane, WA: Egger Publishing.

Sitton, R. (1997). *Spelling Sourcebook Series.* <http://www.sitton spelling.com> (1998, February 19).

Stahl, S.A. (1992). Saying the "p" word: Nine guidelines for exemplary phonics instruction. *The Reading Teacher, 45*(8), 618–625.

Stanovich, K. (1986). Matthew effects in reading: Some consequences of individual differences in the acquisition of literacy. *Reading Research Quarterly, 21,* 360–407.

Stanovich, K.E., Cunningham, A.E., & Cramer, B.B. (1984). Assessing phonological awareness in kindergarten children: Issues of task comparability. *Journal of Experimental Child Psychology, 38*, 175–190.

Stone, J. (1995). *The Animated Alphabet*(™). La Mesa, CA: J. Stone Creations.

Swank, L.K., & Catts, H.W. (1994). Phonological awareness and written decoding. *Language, Speech, and Hearing Services in Schools, 25*, 9–14.

Tarasoff, M. (1990). *Spelling strategies you can teach.* Victoria, BC: Active Learning Institute.

Vacca, J.L., Vacca, R.T., & Gove, M.K. (1991). *Reading and learning to read* (2nd ed.). New York: HarperCollins.

van Kleeck, A., & Bryant, D. (1984, November). *Learning that language is arbitrary: Evidence from early lexical changes.* Paper presented at the meeting of the American Speech-Language-Hearing Association, San Francisco, CA.

Venezky, R.L. (1976). Prerequisites for learning to read. In J.R. Levin & V.L. Allen (Eds.), *Cognitive learning in children: Theories and strategies.* Chestnut Hill, MA: Academic Press.

Vygotsky, L.S. (1962). *Thought and language* (E. Haufman & G. Vakas, Eds. and Trans.). Cambridge, MA: Massachusetts Institute of Technology Press.

Wallach, M., & Wallach, L. (1976). *Teaching all children to read.* Chicago, IL: University of Chicago Press.

Yopp, H. (1988). The validity and reliability of phonemic awareness test. *Reading Research Quarterly, 23*, 159–177.

Yopp, H. (1992). Developing phonemic awareness in young children. *The Reading Teacher, 45*, 696–703.

Yopp, H. (1995a). A test for assessing phonemic awareness in young children. *The Reading Teacher, 29*, 20–29.

Yopp, H. (1995b). Read-aloud books for developing phonemic awareness: An annotated bibliography. *The Reading Teacher, 48*(6), 538–543.

Zhurova, L.E. (1963–1964). The development analysis of words into their sounds by preschool children. *Soviet Psychology and Psychiatry, 17*, 17–27.

Ahlberg, J., & Ahlberg, A. (1978). *Each peach pear plum*. Toronto, ON: Penguin Books Canada.

Ahlberg, J., & Ahlberg, A. (1993). *The jolly postman or other people's letters*. Toronto, ON: Heinneman.

Banatyne-Cugnet, J., & Moore, Y. (1992). *A prairie alphabet*. Montreal, PQ: Tundra Books.

Base, G. (1988). *Animalia*. Toronto, ON: Stoddart.

Birkenshaw-Fleming, L. (1989). *Come on everybody, let's sing!* Toronto, ON: Gordon V. Thompson Music.

Brown, M.W., & Hurd, C. (1975). *Goodnight moon*. New York: Harper Trophy.

Butterworth, N. (1990). *Nick Butterworth's book of nursery rhymes*. New York: Viking.

Cameron, P. (1961). *"I can't," said the ant*. New York: Coward–McCann.

Carle, E. (1974). *The very hungry caterpillar*. Markham, ON: Penguin Puffin Press.

Framst, L.S., & Halliday, S. (1991). *On my walk*. Cecil Lake, BC: Louise Framst.

Hague, K. (1984). *Alphabears*. New York: Henry Holt.

Hawkins, C., & Hawkins. J. (1986). *Tog the dog*. New York: G.P. Putnam's Sons.

Martin, B., & Carle, E. (1992). *Brown bear, brown bear, what do you see?* Markham, ON: Fitzhenry & Whiteside.

Munsch, R. (1980). *The paper bag princess*. Toronto, ON: Annick Press.

Nelson, J.A. (1989). *Lions and gorillas*. Cleveland, OH: Modern Curriculum Press.

Ochs, C.P. (1991). *Moose on the loose*. Minneapolis, MN: Carolrhoda Books.

O'Connor, J., & Alley, R.W. (1986). *The teeny tiny woman*. Toronto, ON: Random House Canada.

Rosen, M., & Oxenburg, H. (1989). *We're going on a bear hunt*. London: Walker Books.

Scarry, R. (1970). *Richard Scarry's best Mother Goose ever*. New York: Western.

Schiller, P., & Moore, T. (1993). *Where is Thumbkin?* Mt. Rainier, MD: Gryphon House.

Children's Book References

Sendak, M. (1991). *Chicken soup with rice*. New York: Harper Trophy.

Seuss, Dr. (1965). *Hop on Pop*. New York: Beginners Books.

Seuss, Dr. (1974). *There's a wocket in my pocket*. New York: Random House.

Tomkins, J. (1987). *When a bear bakes a cake*. Hong Kong, China: Green Tiger Press.

Traponi, I. (1993). *The itsy bitsy spider*. New York: Scholastic.

Warren, J. (1991). *Piggyback songs for school*. Everett, WA: Warren.

MONITORING PROGRESS, 18–24; identification of children with poor phonological awareness, 18–19; tests, 19–24, 85–88, 89–92
MOORE, T., 41
MOORE, Y., 41
MUNSCH, R., 32
MUSIC, 29–31, 39–40

N

NASALS, 66
NELSON, J.A., 41
NICHOLSON, T., 3
NONSENSE SEQUENCE, 37
NURSERY RHYMES, 29, 30, 38–39, 48; sources, 75–79

O

OBSERVATION SURVEY OF EARLY LITERARY ACHIEVEMENT, AN, 69
O'CONNOR, J., 41, 72
ODDITY TASKS, 9
"OLD MCDONALD HAD A FARM," 30, 50, 71
OLOFSSON, A., 1, 5
OLSON, M., 1, 5, 7, 10, 53
ON MY WALK (Framst), 73
OXENBURG, H., 51

P

PARENT LETTERS, 14, 15, 33–34, 42–44, 52, 62–63
"PAW PAW PATCH, THE," 72
PETERS, P.M., 81
PETERSEN, O., 7
PHONEMES, as abstract, 6; initial, 55; isolating, 10, 17, 45–51, 55; listening for, 55
PHONOGRAMS, 67–68, 80
PHONOLOGICAL AWARENESS. See also specific topics; acquisition of, 6; activities, 13, 64–65; child

development and, 3–5; cognitive-linguistic complexity of, 10; definition, 4; levels of, 6–7; reading development and, 5–6; reading success and, 1; resources, 83–84; sequence, 12–17; teachability of, 7–11
PICTURE PUZZLES, 60
POEMS, 14, 15, 29, 38–39, 71; sources, 75–79
POLK, J.K., 23
POOL, J., 67
POSTTEACHING TESTS, 89–92
PRAIRIE ALPHABET (BANATYNE), 41
PRATT, A.C., 5
PRETEACHING TESTS, 19–24, 85–88

R

READING, 1, 5–6, 8
REITERATION, 57, 66
RHYME, 8, 14, 15, 27, 29, 33, 35–41, 48, 71; discrimination of, 36; expressive, 36–37; knowledge of, 36; production of, 36–37; receptive, 36; sources of rhymes, 75–79; test for detection, 19–20, 85, 89
ROBERTSON, C., 19, 23
Role of Phonics in Reading Instruction, The (International Reading Association), 64
Rosen, M., 51
Rosner, J., 8
Roswell-Chall auditory blending test, 21, 90
Routh, D.K., 8, 54, 55

S

SALTER, W., 19, 23
SAWYER, D.J., 32, 38
SCAFFOLDING, 17
SCHUELE, C.M., 5, 28
SEGMENTATION, 10, 17, 22–23, 45,